# SIPAPU

The Story of the Indians of Arizona and New Mexico

# SIPAPU

The Story of the Indians of Arizona and New Mexico

**WILLIAM E. COFFER
(KOI HOSH)**

 VAN NOSTRAND REINHOLD COMPANY
NEW YORK   CINCINNATI   TORONTO   LONDON   MELBOURNE

Manufactured in the United States of America

Published by Van Nostrand Reinhold Company Inc.
135 West 50th Street, New York, N.Y. 10020

Van Nostrand Reinhold Publishing
1410 Birchmount Road
Scarborough, Ontario M1P 2E7, Canada

Van Nostrand Reinhold Australia Pty. Ltd.
17 Queen Street
Mitcham, Victoria 3132, Australia

Van Nostrand Reinhold Company Limited
Molly Millars Lane
Wokingham, Berkshire, England

15 14 13 12 11 10 9 8 7 6 5 4 3 2 1


Library of Congress Cataloging in Publication Data

Coffer, William E.
    Sipapu, the story of the Indians of Arizona and
New Mexico.

    Bibliography: p.
    Includes index.
    1. Indians of North America—Southwest, New—Religion
and mythology. I. Title.
E78.S7C57          299'.799          82-2625
ISBN 0-442-21590-8                   AACR2

*Dedication for SIPAPU:*

*AN OHOYO AIUKLI – VERLA*


*Acknowledgments:*

*To:*

*Cathy Hamlett for her beautiful artwork on the jacket which
enhances the narrative.*


*Marty Hamlett for his support and assistance to Cathy and
his loyalty to me.*


*Tom Sullivan whose spiritual understanding helps keep me
going and his wife, Jeanne, who keeps him going and did
such a marvelous job typing the manuscript.*


*My kids who understood when Dad was too busy to do a
lot of things with them.*


*And finally, my beautiful wife, Verla, for her extreme
patience, understanding, and love which makes all things
possible.*

*Thank you!*

*William E. Coffer (Koi Hosh)*

# Preface

In the mythology of many nations of Indians in the Western Hemisphere are stories describing in detail their emergence from the underground to the surface of the present-day earth. Some of the stories relate upward movement by the people through a succession of worlds. Sometimes these worlds were inhabited by humans in similar form to today's man; other versions speak of spirit forms or of beings of different morphology; and some accounts tell of animals and man coexisting on equal planes.

The Choctaw tell of the emergence of the people of the five great southeastern nations from the confines of the underground at Nanih Waiya, the Sacred Mountain. The Hopi and the Navajo have detailed accounts of their entering this realm in the distant past, coming from worlds beneath this one. The Papago tell how E'etoi, the Elder Brother, molded the original people out of mud in his cave-home in Baboquivre Mountain, and how they left the cave and entered the world.

Kumush, according to the Modoc Indians' oral tradition, went to the underground world of spirits and brought out bones to make the many tribes of Indians.

Perhaps more than any other group of Indians, the Pueblo people perpetuate the emergence story both in their oral tradition and, in symbolism, in the construction of their ceremonial houses, or kivas. They believe they originated inside the earth where their spirit Mother resides. Various types of beings were there and, when the time to enter this world came about, the animals, birds, and insects helped the people come through the underground worlds and enter this one. They emerged at Sipapu, which is north of present-day Peubloland, but they could not remain there for it was too sacred for humans. The people moved southward and, because of internal quarreling and bickering, broke up into small bands and became the various tribal groups.

The Pueblo people, however, did not forget Sipapu, the place of their beginning. In every kiva built by them, they construct a sipapu hole in the floor to remind them of this sacred place. In every ceremonial house of these pueblo dwellers is found a small two- to three-inch diameter hole drilled into the earth to symbolize this memorial occasion. The spirits which still dwell under the earth are thought to enter the kiva through the sipapu during ceremonies to sanctify the activities.

This publication is titled *Sipapu* with the anticipation that the spirits will enter it and bless it. It is hoped they will give the reader comprehension of the southwestern Indians and establish an affinity which will eradicate racial, cultural, and societal obstacles between all peoples.

Yakoke cha imola,
Koi Hosh

# Introduction

Before embarking on a study of the native inhabitants of a particular geographic area such as the Southwest, it is appropriate that the boundaries of that portion of land be identified. This poses an almost impossible task when dealing with American Indians, for their use of the land as hunting or agricultural "homelands" depended not on maps or fences, but rather on traditional occupancy and agreement, sometimes strongly contested, with neighboring groups. This is especially true in the Southwest because of the diversity of the people and cultures existing there.

Since these boundaries have been a source of debate among scholars for years, we will reflect the author's definition of the confines of the Southwest. This includes the states of Arizona and New Mexico in their entirety as the primary area, with slight extrusions into western Texas, southern Colorado, and Utah. The Colorado River forms the division line on the western edge. While many of the tribes extend far beyond these delineations, the discussion in this publication will be limited for the most part to this description of the Southwest. This area contains the largest concentration of native American Indians in the United States, and many of these nations are occupying territory on which their ancestors lived for centuries.

The history texts used in most schools in the United States blatantly state that St. Augustine, Florida is the oldest permanently inhabited city in North America. Yet many Indian communities were aged when St. Augustine was established. Irrefutable scientific evidence in the form of dendrochronology (tree-ring dating), indicates the town of Oraibi has clung tenaciously to the side of the 600-foot high cliffs of third Mesa for over 1100 years. Other cities throughout the country, although many were renamed as the Europeans took possession after ruthlessly driving the Indians away, were inhabited long before Columbus "discovered" America. Wherever areas were found which were strategically located with facilities especially suited for agriculture or commerce, the Indian communities were replaced by white settlements. It was then, and only then, that "history" began for that city.

Common usage of the word "prehistory" by learned anthropologists, historians, and other academicians to refer to the prewhite era in America seems rather ludicrous, for history literally began at the moment time began. Their reference appears egocentric to this author, for what is generally meant by this term in American Indian associations, is pre-European history or prewhite history. It does not seem appropriate to begin "history" in 1492.

The Southwest contains many of these "prehistoric" cities including a number of the Rio Grande Pueblos, Acoma, as well as villages on most of the contemporary Indian reservations. Cities such as Tucson, Phoenix, Coolidge, and other centers of population were Indian villages long before Coronado made his journey into the area in 1540. Most of these were developed by members of the four basic prewhite cultures — Anasazi, Hohokam, Mogollon, and Athapaskan. The latter, though their arrival in the area barely predates that of the whites, must be considered separately because of their distinctive cultural attributes. Subgroups in the other three primary cultures illustrate a great deal of diversity, but for general purposes in this manuscript they will be considered as branches of the "mother group."

This author, having traveled for years in nearly every nook and cranny of the Southwest, offers a personalized presentation of the people of the area, not as museum specimens or as inanimate subjects of study, but as living peoples and cultures moving vibrantly across the deserts and mountains of this enchanting geographic area.

To the white man this land of sand and rocks, unfriendly plants, and extremes of heat and cold, inhabited by poverty-stricken people may seem inhospitable and anything but enchanted. Yet, to the tribespeople of the nations who inhabit it, the great Southwest is home. Geronimo expressed it quite succinctly when he said after years of exile:

> For each tribe of men Usen created, He also made a home. In the land for any particular tribe He placed whatever would be best for the welfare of that tribe.
>
> When Usen created the Apaches He also gave them their homes in the West. He gave them such grain, fruits, and game as they needed to eat . . . He gave them a pleasant climate and all they needed for clothing and shelter was at hand.
>
> Thus it was in the beginning:  The Apaches and their homes, each created for the other by Usen Himself. When they are taken from these homes they sicken and die.*

Geronimo spoke of a typical Indian characteristic, his love for his homeland. This aesthetic emotion of mystical identification with the land is usually unfathomable to the white man, for he cannot view the environment from an Indian perspective. To him, it is real estate, ready either to be exploited or abandoned. To the Indian, it is home, the place of creation for his people, the earth which contains the sacred bones of his ancestors. Thus, it is in reality a part of himself.

It is with the utmost respect and reverence that this author tells the story of the Indians of the Southwest.

---

*William E. Coffer  *The Indian Historian,*  "Genocide of the California Indians" (San Francisco:  American Indian Historical Society, 1977) p. 8.

# Contents

Ancient Kiva.  Note sipapu below firepit in lower center indicated by arrow

# SIPAPU

The Story of the Indians of Arizona and New Mexico

# 1
# The Early Southwesterners

Long before the white-eyed, bearded strangers brought their hairy, smelly bodies to the Southwest seeking the riches of the lands, many civilizations and cultures had come and gone. Some had evolved into the tribes the Spaniards found in the sixteenth century, while others seemingly disappeared into the vast deserts and mountains where they remain until this day, one of the many secrets this area still holds. Indian people know that they have lived on their land far longer than written history records, far longer than anyone can remember, back to the origins of man as related in their creation stories.[1]  Much of their history is found in the myths passed from generation to generation through oral tradition.[2]

Archaeologists have also contributed greatly to the knowledge of life-styles and cultural attributes of the "Ancient Ones" of the Southwest by their arduous and meticulous excavations and analysis of habitation sites.  The basic cultural divisions must be considered if we are to totally comprehend the people of today.

### EARLIEST KNOWN MAN

Although it is recognized that man has been in the Southwest for a very long time, the extent of his presence is still a debatable question. Located adjacent to the area we are discussing, and undoubtedly affecting the length of time of human habitation in Arizona and New Mexico, is the archaeological excavation in the Calico Mountains near Barstow, California.

In the 1950s, Ruth D. Simpson directed a survey of the Lake Manix area in the Mojave Desert of California. She found evidence which led her to believe that the area had been inhabited by humans during a time period far predating any other found in the New World. She was successful in arousing the interest of Dr. Louis S. B. Leakey, archaeologist famed for his work in Africa, in the project. He came to Calico and began directing the excavation, the only such activity ever attempted by Dr. Leakey in the Americas.

The efforts at Calico produced stone tools much older than any previously discovered. Dr. Leakey identified crude choppers and other implements which he dated 50,000 to 75,000 years ago. Later discoveries have moved the dating back to about 100,000 years.[3] This far predates any other accepted dating of material, and has initiated heated controversy among archaeologists. Also, because of the acid condition of the soil in Calico, no human fossils have been found. This leaves a gap of 70,000 to 80,000 years between Calico man and the oldest human bones found in America. This fact only adds fuel to the flames of the conflict.

About 12,000 to 13,000 years ago the first known people about whose existence there is no controversy, occupied the Southwest. They were a hunting group and most of our information about them comes from kill sites of large animals. These people were nomadic hunters who roamed about leaving little in the way of remains. We only know that they had shaped projectile points which were used for hunting and bone tools used for utilitarian purposes around their camps.

As time passed, these groups of hunters began to supplement their meat diet by gathering wild plant food. These gatherers

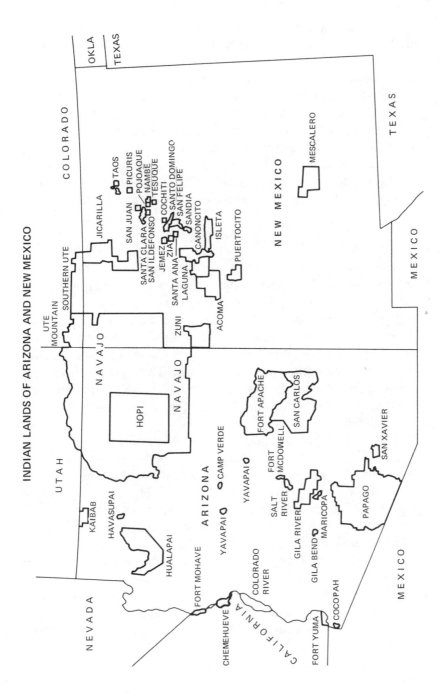

INDIAN LANDS OF ARIZONA AND NEW MEXICO

evolved into the Desert culture, best represented in our area of discussion by the Cochise culture, which flourished about 7000 years ago. The Cochise people placed more importance on grinding stones than on stone points, which indicates a change from a hunting to a gathering society. During the centuries of existence of the Cochise culture, little change is indicated in the way of life until about 200–300 B.C. when new cultural traits began to appear. These changes were in the form of the introduction of corn from Mexico, construction of housing, use of pottery, burial of the dead and other innovations that brought about cultural changes which can be directly linked to current Indian tribal units.

## MOGOLLON

Around 300 B.C. a new culture began to appear in the mountainous area of today's western New Mexico and eastern Arizona. Definite connections have been made between this new entity and the Cochise culture, but there were such new features as formalized and rather elaborate structures and pottery. Food gathering continued and primitive agriculture was indicated in the growing of corn, beans, and squash. These plants played an ever-increasing part in the economy of these people, but it took several hundred years before the full potential of corn was realized.

This new cultural group is called Mogollon because of its general geographic location along the Mogollon Rim, the southern escarpment of a mountainous chain extending from southwestern New Mexico to northwestern Arizona. The early Mogollon built their houses on ridges or terraces above streams, probably because they were easier to defend, but also because the limited farmland was too precious to be used for housing.

The earliest Mogollon pottery seems to be well made with no evolutionary periods. This would indicate that it was developed by some other group and "borrowed" by the Mogollon. It is probable that it was introduced from Mexico, for it is quite similar, especially in the use of a red surface finish, to that found there in the same period.

Housing consisted of rather large circular pit houses in loosely knit villages. Each house had a short entrance area, usually a center post and a fire pit. Located in each of these clusters of houses was a large structure, some being as much as thirty to thirty-five feet in diameter, which served as a ceremonial house, or kiva. These kivas were present throughout the Mogollon culture period, therefore they predate the better-known Anasazi kivas by hundreds of years.[4]

Artifacts indicate a highly developed culture which evolved over the centuries until the peaceful invasion of the Anasazi from the north began to erode the Mogollon culture. By about A.D. 1200, or a little later, the Mogollon culture disappeared as an identifiable entity, and the only descendants left by this group seem to be the Zuni Indians of western New Mexico.

### HOHOKAM

The development of Hohokam culture in its early stages is clearly linked with that of the Mogollon. Since both came from the Cochise culture, they were quite similar in the beginning. However, since the Mogollon were mountain-dwelling people and the Hohokam developed as a desert culture, they soon took on very distinct and different attributes.

Instead of pit houses, the Hohokam built houses within pits, not using the earthen walls as an integral part of the house itself. They also practiced cremation as a funerary method which further differentiated them from the Mogollon. Although both groups originated as divisions of the Cochise about 300 B.C., by the time of Christ they had developed quite different ways of life.

The Hohokam culture had become almost totally agricultural by A.D. 300 and depended on irrigation of their desert homeland in southern Arizona to ensure successful harvests of crops. They developed an intricate system of canals and floodgates which enabled them to "make the desert bloom." Modern engineering with its sophisticated equipment has not been able to improve the original canals except to cement the banks to retard erosion.

In three or four hundred more years the Hohokam had reached its peak of development. Ball courts "borrowed" from Mexico were prevalent, and irrigation systems had been improved with some of the canals reaching as far as thirty miles into the desert. Excellent shell and stone implements and ornaments were developed and some of their artistry, such as etching in shell, placed them far ahead of their European counterparts.

Hohokam artisans produced varied and unusual products during the peak periods of the culture. Mirrors were made from thin slices of iron pyrite carefully fitted together. How this was accomplished is still a mystery for pyrite crystals are usually cubic and extremely hard. Stone vessels were ornate and exotic in form. These art objects were used as funerary offerings for the dead and were placed in the ashes either at the burn-site or in the repositories made for the ashes.

Beginning at about A.D. 1200, groups of Anasazi began moving into the Gila and Salt River Valleys, the home of the Hohokam. The two cultures lived together peacefully, each holding tenaciously to its own life-style, sometimes even cohabiting the same villages. The Hohokam lived in their pit houses while their neighbors occupied apartments. The Anasazi buried their dead and the Hohokam continued their practice of cremation. Each group's pottery kept the individualized styles and patterns of the particular culture which made it.

For a period of about one hundred years, from about the mid-1400 to the mid-1500s, there is no archaeological record of the Hohokam people. They seem to have just disappeared. When the Spanish reached the area in 1540 and found the Pima and Papago Indians and the ruins of the previous culture, they inquired who had developed such a civilization. The Indians replied that it was the Hohokam, "those who have gone away." What was not explained was the story in the oral tradition of both tribes of where they went.

It tells of an exodus by the Hohokam from their homeland, a period of wandering throughout the northern part of Mexico, and an eventual return to their original homes.[5]

Casa Grande Natural Monument, Coolridge Arizona

## ANASAZI

There is no precise delineation as to when a culture begins or ends, only estimations of time. Such is the case with the Anasazi cultural period, for from about 5000 B.C. until today, the Anasazi traditions were carried on by Indians.

For the first 5000 years or so, man lived in the Four Corners area and left artifacts which indicate a simple gathering culture. These high-plateau dwellers were probably distantly related to the Cochise people discussed earlier. They have been assigned the name of "Basket Makers" because of their use of woven utensils. Basket Maker I is the name for the period from 5000 B.C. to about the time of Christ. The people are called "Anasazi," the Ancient Ones, by the Navajo.

From about 100 B.C. to about A.D. 500, the culture became widespread throughout the plateau area. Some agriculture developed during this period, but it was extensively supplemented by gathering and hunting. The Anasazi used the atlatl, a wooden implement which provides increased power in spear throwing, but they did not have the bow and arrow. They sometimes lived in caves, used storage pits, had no pottery, and constructed a few circular log houses.

From A.D. 500 to about 700 innovations began to appear, some self-developed but many which were introduced by the Mogollon culture from the south. Beans became a new staple item in the diet and permanent housing was started. Pottery was made and the bow and arrow found its way into the culture replacing the spear and atlatl.

By about A.D. 700 to 900 the Basket Maker progressed to a point that archaeologists name the period Pueblo I. Housing had become more tightly clustered, pottery was being made with more imagination, and true ceremonial houses (kivas) began to appear. Even the physical characteristics of the people were beginning to change from a long head to a round one.

By about A.D. 900 to 1100, the Anasazi began to be more sophisticated in many aspects. Pottery became more colorful and bold in design. A "population boom" seems to have

Mesa Verde National Park in Colorado

occurred about this time which did not make the villages larger, but did lend to a proliferation of them in canyons and mesas that had not been previously occupied. Nearly every village had its kiva for ceremonial purposes.

For some unknown reason the Anasazi began to group together in the period A.D. 1100 to 1300 and construct larger, multistoried houses. Pottery, basketry, weaving, jewelry, architecture, and art reached new heights during this time. Trade and travel increased and commerce was conducted with neighboring units at an increasing rate.

The Anasazi also had serious problems during the years from A.D. 1276 to A.D. 1299, for no rain fell in the region. People began to move out of their established cities at Mesa Verde, Chaco Canyon, Aztec, and the many other cultural centers in search of water. By around A.D. 1300 the entire San Juan drainage basin in the Four Corners area had been abandoned. The Anasazi spread throughout the Rio Grande valley, south into Mogollon country, and, as indicated earlier, even to the land of the Hohokam.

During the next period, 1300 to 1598, the balance of the northern Anasazi moved southward and joined their long-established relatives, the Hopi and Zuni. Larger villages became the norm as more and more people congregated in village areas where there was water. There was a lack of progress during this time in such areas as architecture and pottery, and more emphasis was placed on spiritual matters. Religious activities, as depicted in the murals on the kiva walls, reached a new height, and art, ornamentation, and commercial trade were highlighted. It was not necessarily a regressive period, but one of reorientation.

Although the Spanish had been present in the area in 1540 when Coronado's expedition traversed the region, it was not until 1598, when the missionaries, soldiers, and settlers arrived, that the Pueblo (Anasazi) felt the Spanish impact. The years from 1598 to today have been the great period of change for them. Pressures from European and American powers have forced the people into a dual-world situation. They function

Grand Kiva at Aztec National Monument, New Mexico

Wapatki National Monument, Arizona — Large Anasazi Ruins

Ancient Kiva at Wapatki National Monument

in the modern era of time because of economic necessity, while at the same time they maintain much of the traditional religious attitudes of the "Ancient Ones," the Anasazi.

## OTHER SOUTHWESTERN CULTURES

Although three primary cultural groups who inhabited the Southwest prior to the coming of the Europeans have been outlined, this does not suggest that there were not many more cultures and subcultures present. A few of these are illustrated to demonstrate the variety and wide diversity of the people in this region.

In northern Arizona have been found many remains of a group of people who were contemporaneous with the Anasazi. Because of the many common traits, they were probably branches of the basic Anasazi culture. However, since they also reflect traits of the Mogollon, the name Sinagua (the Spanish word for "without water") has been assigned to them. These people were agriculturists who planted their crops in low areas and did not depend on irrigation, hence their name.

The northern group of Sinaguans are represented by the ruins around Flagstaff, Arizona. During the great drought years, many of them left the area and moved south to the Hohokam territory. Some Sinaguans had already established Wapatki, but were forced out when no rain fell. The entire northern branch had evacuated the area by about A.D. 1300.

Some people built large pueblos along the Verde River at Tuzigoot and Montezuma's Castle. Others probably moved on and joined the Indians of the Little Colorado River area and were the ancestors of the present Hopi Indians.

The Patayan culture was located along the Colorado River below the Grand Canyon before the arrival of the white man. There were many of these people in the area when it was visited by Father Eusebio Kino, a Jesuit priest, about 1700.[6] It is likely that by then they had evolved from the gathering society of Patayan, a Walapai word meaning "the Old People," to the current cultures represented by the Yuman-speaking tribes.

The Patayans built large masonry structures such as forts, granaries, and pit houses. Most of their building sites have been

Walnut Canyon National Monument, Arizona

Montezuma's Castle National Monument, Arizona

obliterated by the annual overflowing of the river and by the construction of dams and lakes along the Colorado. Perhaps in the future some door will open which will enable us to learn more details about the Patayan culture.

Another enigma surrounds the migration and time of arrival in the Southwest of the Athapaskan people. Closely related culturally and linguistically with the natives of the Alaskan interior and the Yukon, there is no consensus among archaeologists as to their time of arrival or their migration route. It is generally agreed that they are comparative newcomers to the Southwest, arriving not too long before the Spanish. These Athapaskan people are the Navajo and Apache we know today, and their presence in the area greatly affected the lives of most inhabitants.

One branch moved into the Pueblo region, and their raiding tactics gained them their Pueblo name Navajo meaning "enemies of the cultivated fields." Being very adaptive people, they synthesized their culture and borrowed much from other groups. They adopted sheep and goats from the Spanish along with ornate silverwork, and from the Pueblo they learned agriculture and weaving. These new cultural acquisitions became so ingrained in Navajo culture that, even today, they are the basics of Navajo economics.

Other groups of the Athapaskan moved further east and south and became known as Apache, a Zuni word meaning "enemy." These nomadic warriors were harassed by the Spanish and some Indian tribes to such an extent that they were forced in self-defense to develop a raiding culture. They became the scourge of the Southwest as a result. The Apache were never given the opportunity to become sedentary, for they were always pressured by someone, and this is what brought them their infamous reputation from the White Mountains in Arizona to far south into Sonora, Mexico.

These diverse cultural aspects of the groups illustrated establishes the "roots" and identity of the tribal units discussed in the balance of this book. By acquiring a knowledge of the prewhite cultures located in the Southwest, it is now easier to comprehend the diversity of culture and languages found in contemporary time.

2

# Papago or Papavi O'Otam

Excavation by Dr. Emil Haury of the University of Arizona at Ventana Cave near Santa Rosa on the Papago Reservation tell the story of man's existence in that area of the Southwest for over 10,000 years. Evidence found by Haury's group shows habitation of the cave dating from the Desert culture, through the Cochise period, and until the end of the Hohokam era.

The lowest levels of the cave contained the bones of now extinct animals which were once hunted by the inhabitants. The people who consumed the animals were primarily hunters and gatherers. Projectile points, scrapers, bone awls, and other implements were found which indicate that wild animals were killed and prepared for food and clothing. Various grinding and milling tools show that the people gathered wild seeds and roots and pulverized them to make them edible. There is no evidence at this level of Ventana Cave to suggest that there was any form of pottery or that the Indians practiced any agriculture.[7]

In the next stage of evolution, as shown by a change in the type of artifacts found, corn and pottery were used beginning about A.D. 100. This period marks the beginning of a sedentary agricultural population indicating the demise of the Cochise and the start of the Hohokam culture. This new lifeway continued in the cave throughout the Hohokam period until about 1400–50.

Besides corn and pottery, archaeologists found human mummies, cotton cloth, woven sandals, and well-made baskets. New objects were found in strata that indicated the placement corresponded to the general Hohokam development in the area. The ruins at Casa Grande National Monument near Coolidge, Arizona represent one of the final stages of the Hohokam culture. Little archaeological evidence is available for the period 1450 to 1698 when Father Kino entered the area. What little evidence there is suggests that there was a direct cultural continuity between the Hohokam and the present-day Papago.

A new phase of history was introduced when Father Kino began visiting Papagueria, for he brought many new ideas and introduced better farming methods. He started the Indians raising cattle, an industry which still provides a stable economic unit for them. The good padre carried grapevines and attempted to show the people how to develop vineyards. Little success was realized in this venture, for the climate was not suited for grapes.

The Papago cultivated fields, growing beans, corn, and squash along the intermittent streams during the summer months when the rains came to provide moisture for the crops. After the crops were harvested, the people moved to the mountains where the springs were located, and hunted and gathered wild food products to sustain them through the winter. Thus, each local group had two homes and divided their time between them. Some of the old Papago still adhere to this custom.[8] The villages were rather small and never had the population or size of the pueblos. Even today they follow the same pattern and generally consist of only a few houses in any one site, usually those of the clan or family group. Some 149 separate and distinct locations on the main reservation have been identified as settlements. Of these only 10 have a population of over one hundred today. These major villages are Ali Chukson, Hickiwan, Topawa, Quijotoa, Gu Achi, Gu Vo, Pisinimo, Gu Oidak, Chuichu, and Sells.[9]

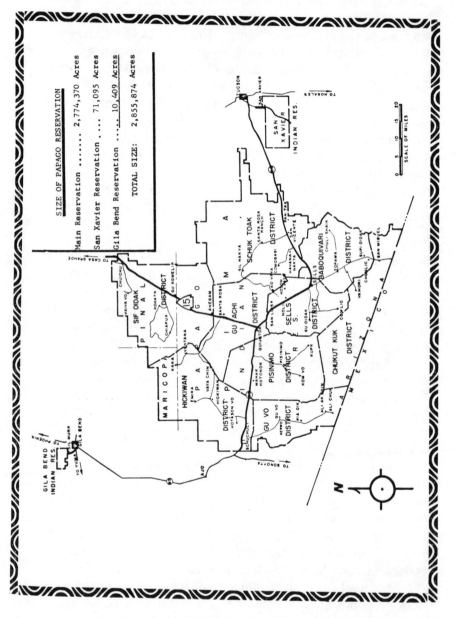

The Papago Reservations.

The most important political unit of the Papago was the village. Each was independent and, until the United States imposed jurisdiction on the Papago, there was never any general tribal organization under a single leader. Each village had two ceremonial houses, one in the summer location and one in the winter village. The house was circular, made of brush, and called the Rain or Cloud House. The sacred fetishes which each village kept could only be opened on ceremonial occasions in the Rain House. These houses served much as the Pueblo kivas, for it was here that, besides ceremonial uses, the men met regularly to handle the village governmental matters and to discuss general problems.

The meetings of the men in the Rain House were presided over by a village patriarch who was called the Keeper of the Smoke, a title indicative of his duty of building a fire before each meeting. He was not only in charge of the secular meetings, but also was the leader of village ceremonies for rain and ritual purification. There were other specially designated men who were leaders in their particular activities such as the hunt, the games and races, the war parties, and the ceremonial singing. Each of these men had many ritual duties in connection with his leadership and all were subject to the resolutions of the council of elders who made the ultimate decision on any matter which affected the village.

Although most Indian nations are organized under a matriarchal and matrilineal system, the Papago are patriarchal and patrilineal. These patrilineal families are grouped into two larger units (clans), one called Buzzards and the other Coyotes. These clans regulated marriage within the tribe, and there could be no intermarriage within either group. This would have been considered an incestual relationship and carried severe punishment for the participants. Although Papago clans did not have the strong social structure as evidenced in some tribal units in the Southwest, the marriage control was strongly enforced.

Thus, Papago social organization was based on small autonomous village units governed in a democratic manner by officials who were ritual rather than political leaders. This type of

leadership prevailed until the passage of the Indian Reorganization Act in 1934. Under the provisions of this legislation, tribal
governments were established on a political basis.

Today the basic political document which governs the Papago
Tribe is the *Constitution and By Laws of the Papago Tribe,
Arizona,* ratified by tribal members on December 12, 1936, and
approved by the Secretary of the Interior on January 6, 1937.
The governing body of the tribe is an elected tribal council consisting of twenty-two members, two from each of the eleven
districts of the reservation.  Council meetings are held each
month and are presided over by a chairman elected by the
council members.  Each district is a local governing body which
selects its own district council.  These districts are quite large
geographically and when combined, present nearly three million
acres of land to be governed.

Most of this vast expanse is nonproductive except as range-
land for the tribe's cattle herd.  Since rainfall is so slight and
vegetation so sparse, one square mile produces only enough
grazing for three head of livestock. The Papago have attempted
to improve both their pasture and their cattle, but with almost
perpetual drought, even scientific cattle-raising methods are less
than successful in providing adequate income for the project.

In spite of severe overgrazing and the heavy drought losses
almost every year, this principal livelihood on the reservation
produces an annual income of over $2 million for the Papago
stock owners and the tribe.  Per capita income for the reservation, however, was only $807 in 1973, one of the lowest of any
tribe of Indians in America. The future doesn't seem too bright
for succeeding years.  In spite of spiraling inflation, the per
capita income increased only $5.00 per person to the amount of
$812 in 1974, and is far below the national poverty level today.

Many Papago still must leave the reservation each year to
seek work in the cities.  There are permanent colonies of the
people in Tucson, Phoenix, Ajo, and other southern Arizona
communities.  The Papago find it extremely difficult to abandon
their old ways and adopt those of the dominant society, and
most do not want to do so. Money motivation, for instance, is

still an alien idea to most Papago families. The materialistic value system they must face in the cities is a frightening and frustrating experience. An old Papago is quoted as saying, "Perhaps the Papago people have been tied to the old too long and exposed to the new too soon." Although to the casual observer they seem to live in modern-day America, those who know the Papago people realize their roots are grounded in their specialized Sonoran Catholicism and their traditional way of life. Very few Papago become permanent residents of the urban setting and are constantly returning home for some "Papagoizing"; and after being rejuvenated, they go back to the city in order to provide their families with the means for economic survival.

Spiritual and philosophical survival though, is where the traditions of the people still rule the Papago. In most of the villages there is an adobe building with a cross over the door — the Sonoran Catholic Church. Sonoran Catholicism is far older than any of the other Christian religions on the Papago Reservation. It originated when Father Kino and other Jesuit priests came among them about the turn of the eighteenth century. After the expulsion of the Jesuits from the New World in 1767, the Papago spent many generations with no clergy. During this time they developed a form of Catholicism which they could embrace without compromising their traditional religion.

When Catholic missionaries again visited Papagueria in the late 1800s, they were presented with a "new" form of the Church. Much of the creed and ritual had vanished and a more casual and informal approach was used. In the Sonoran Catholic Church, as it was called later, there was no mass, no hymns or prayers in Latin, no confession, and no marriage ceremony. Children were baptized by their godparents and the people buried their own dead. The Desert People like to manage their own affairs and were very clear in relating this to Rome.

The Roman Catholic Church, realizing that it must "bend," or lose the Papago altogether, exhibited great flexibility and agreed to "allow" the Papago to have a special branch of the Catholic religion. Consequently, the fact that their religion is largely self-conducted and does not conflict drastically with

San Xavier Mission near Tucson, Arizona on the Papago Indian Reservation

their traditional spiritual concepts is the chief reason for the Catholic Church's hold on the Papago. Today the reservation population is about eighty-five percent Sonoran Catholic. This allows the priests not only to have a strong influence on the spiritual lives of the people, but also on the secular affairs of the reservation. However, although they are devout Sonoran Catholics, the Papago still hold their traditional ceremonies as they have for centuries. As with most Indians, especially in the Southwest where the difference between physical chaos and physical survival is slight, the religious practices of the O'otam are centered around the recurring events of the annual economic cycle. The regular ceremonial events include a festival in early summer when the saguaro cactus fruit is gathered, a deer dance in autumn when the people come back from the field villages, and rain dances in the spring before the cactus fruit ripens. In addition to these annual ceremonies and dances, every four years a very special ceremony is held. It is called Viikita and is regarded as a harvest festival.

The Viikita is an elaborate ceremony in which most of the important elements of Papago ritual can be found. It requires the cooperation of several villages and a long period of preparation. The men of each village work for ten days making effigies to represent mythical beings or places and large quantities of feathered prayersticks are assembled. Each village sends a group of singers with their leader and each of these leaders compose new songs for the occasion. Masked clowns, similar to the clown kachinas of Pueblo ceremonies, take part in the celebration. These comical personages hold their office through inheritance, as do most of the other ceremonial participants. The Viikita ceremony includes the singing of songs while the effigies are carried in procession, symbolic representations of the sun and the moon, sprinkling of cornmeal, and representation of parts of the Papago flood myth.

Some of the lesser ceremonies held by villages or even individuals include ritual drinking of the sacred wine. These are generally observed as "cleansing" or "purification" rites.[10]

Oral tradition also plays an important part of Papago native religion. The modern-day Papago child receives the same oral instruction as his ancestors and the stories are kept alive.[11] Boys in traditional Papago homes practice running and still receive their visions as animals come to sing to them when they fall, exhausted from a long run across the desert. Each boy must learn the magic powers the animal confers on him. If he is attentive he will understand how to acquire food in the desert, for the animals know the secrets. He will also know how to escape enemies, for the animals know, and how to cure diseases and, as the animals sing to the boy and the boy learns the songs, he acquires the magic of the singer. Whatever the youth learns from the animals will be his most precious possession throughout his life. Therefore, running is extremely important to these desert people.

Girls are not expected to have visions like this, but they are taught to work hard, for no man wants a lazy woman for a wife. Just as the boys are taught the skills of trade by their fathers and grandfathers, the girls are instructed in homemaking skills by the mothers and grandmothers. These instructions are recited every morning beginning while the children are quite young, too young to understand, but when they grow up, they have the teachings firmly in mind.

Although acculturation processes have been at work on the Papago intermittently since about 1700 through religious organizations, schools, and governmental agencies, they have not totally "taken." It is true that most young Papago speak English, for this is necessary for their forced school attendance. It is also a fact that these seemingly acculturated children speak their native language fluently and use it almost exclusively at home. They attend services at their Christian churches, but also are totally dedicated to the native religion and use the "white man's religion" more as a social activity than a spiritual one.

The Papago people have enjoyed relative isolation from the dominant society until recent times. Although the San Xavier Reservation near Tucson was established in 1874 and the small Gila Bend Reservation in 1883, the Sells Reservation where most of the people live was not set aside until 1917. This was the original homeland of the Papago, and since it is so barren and inhospitable to most non-Papago, except for a few anthropologists, ministers, and Bureau of Indian Affairs employees, the people were left pretty much to themselves. This enabled many facets of their traditional ways to remain undisturbed.

Even today in Papago homes where a birth is imminent, both parents are careful not to do anything that will bring bad luck. The father does not fight or hunt, for he must be careful not to kill at this time. If he were to fight, he would not have any strength and he might be killed himself. Just before the child is to arrive, the mother removes herself from the home and goes to a special house for women. It is thought that such a strange thing as birth has supernatural power and should not take place in the family house. In times past, the woman would stay in this special house for a month with her women relatives caring for her. Modern times have changed this to some degree and the period of isolation is much shorter. Some of the younger mothers even go to the Indian Health Service hospital to have their children. Traditionally though, the mother stays in the birth house until the moon has gone around "to where it was before." At that time the new mother takes the infant to the medicine man for a kind of baptism.

The husband accompanies the wife and at sunrise the ceremony begins. The medicine man mixes some yellow clay in a small bowl and marks the mother and baby. He then gives some of the clay to the parents and the child to eat. While all of this is taking place, the medicine man sings special songs, some of which are traditional and some that are composed especially for this service. These songs remove the strangeness of birth from the mother and baby and make it possible for them to go back and live with the other people.

During the ritual, the medicine man also gives the baby a name which has been revealed to him in a magical dream. These names have special significance for the child and are never used. Instead, the children are referred to by terms of relationship, such as "my younger sister" or "my sister's child." As they grow older they are given nicknames which are freely used.

Shrine of the Children — Papago Indian Reservation, Arizona

Sacred Wine House — Papago Indian Reservation, Arizona

As the child grows, it becomes an integral part of the everyday life of the family, first toddling about emulating the activities of the other members and then, as maturation continues, doing chores and learning the proper behavior expected from an adult Papago.

It is the grandparents who provide most of the training for the children, for the young parents are busy with the work necessary to provide for the family. In the evening, after the meal, the grandfather talks, telling stories and giving instruction on social behavior.[12]   Even more effective is the teaching in the early hours of morning while it is still dark. Grandfather begins talking in a low gentle voice, telling the children how they must always work and never be lazy, for it is only hard work that enables the people to survive. This sort of speech is recited every morning beginning while the children are too young to understand so that, as they grow up, they have the concepts firmly embedded in their minds. This is one of the surest methods of perpetuating the traditional lifeways of the Papago people.

Papago, however, realize that they must evolve and keep pace with the changing world if they are to survive economically as a tribe. Many innovations have been adapted by them which, only by careful selection of priorities and by tenacity in retaining their tradition whenever possible, allow them to improve their economic position and still be "Papago." Such operations as a solar energy complex located in the western portion of the reservation are a gigantic intrusion into the modern technological world. The tribe has initiated the Papago Tribal Range Water Development Program, spending over $3.5 million on range rehabilitation and water conservation. Mining interests are being promoted and, since the Papago obtained underground mineral rights to their reservation in 1953, the products from the enormous copper deposits are starting to substantially strengthen their economy.

Old traditional skills are still practiced among the Papago and some of these bring monetary rewards. There has been a resurgence of interest in making and marketing the beautiful

Papago baskets which are now found in nearly every "Indian" store in the country. Papago pottery, retaining the rather primitive appearance of ancient pottery, is now becoming popular. The tribe operates an Arts and Crafts Cooperative at Sells, the tribal headquarters, which encourages the finest in workmanship and design among the artisans because of the premium prices offered for top-quality merchandise. Other activities bring income to the tribal treasury but the Papago people still are victims of poverty and, despite the brightening future, unemployment and underemployment are still quite high.

Acceptable ways of economically developing both the material and human resources will continue to be explored. As self-determination becomes a more apparent reality, perhaps the O'otam, the Desert People, the Papago, will attain their rightful place of respect and economic security in society without having to sacrifice their beautiful and rich cultural heritage.

# 3
# Pima and Maricopa

The Pima are descendants of the Hohokam, and their early cultural history has been described in Chapters 1 and 2. General pre-white attributes of the Patayan culture, from which the Maricopa Indians evolved, are also explained in Chapter 1. Therefore, this chapter will address the more contemporary activities of these two groups which, although diverse in language and customs, have lived harmoniously together for a long period of time.

Originally the Maricopa lived between the Gila and the Colorado Rivers where they were in constant conflict with the Yuma, Cocopa, and other tribes of the area. The exact time of their departure from the Colorado River Territory is unknown and presents quite a controversy in historical circles. They were encountered by Juan de Oñate in 1604–05 as he made his historic exploration of the Southwest. In the 1690s, Father Kino visited the Maricopa, but by this time they had migrated to the Gila River area and were living at the western boundary of the Pima.

Sometime during their migration from the lower Colorado River, the Maricopa absorbed the Halchidoma, Kavelchadom, and other small Yuma tribes that lived along the rivers. The Maricopa, already a conglomerate group, joined the Opa, who had already migrated, and the Pima who were the original inhabitants. Thus, by the early 1700s there was a heavily mixed society living in the Gila River Valley. Since this time, the history of these people has become so mingled that it is virtually impossible to identify individual groups.[13] Therefore, in this book, they will be considered under the rubric of Pima.

The name "Pima" itself came into being in a rather comical manner over two hundred years ago. Spaniards, as they traveled around southern Arizona, asked the Indians many questions. The Indians thought it wise not to talk too much, so they answered all inquiries with "pi nyi meach", which means "I do not know." The Spaniards assumed this as the identifying words for the tribe and began calling them "Pima." They call themselves O'otam, or to distinguish themselves from the Papago, O'otam Akimalt, meaning "River People."

Both the Pima and Papago speak dialects of the great Uto-Aztecan linguistic family and can converse with one another. Other speakers of the same language division, because of dialectic differences and geographic separation for long periods of time, do not have this ability. The Pima have been exposed to the acculturation process as long as any group in the Southwest. Even with that exposure to the Spanish, Mexican, and finally, the Americans, because of their resolute nature and because the whites were only interested in the water, not the land, the Pima still retain many facets of their traditional culture. Songs, dances, stories, and other portions of the "old ways" are still very much alive today.

Architecture is still very functional, as it is with most Indians, having evolved into the most suitable style of abode for their particular environment. Today many Pima families live in "sandwich" houses with adobe walls stripped inside and out with one-by-four lumber to strengthen and support the mud. These dwellings are generally covered with sheets of corrugated metal or by boards covered with tar paper. Much of the housing is less elaborate and many homes are mere shacks. The economic status of the tribe precludes fancy homes and most Pima people are comfortable in their traditional houses. Nearly every yard contains a ramada, a brush-covered frame in which much of the cooking, eating, and other family activities take place in the summer months.

In the traditional villages, or family housing groups, there is one more house, small and set aside from the rest of the structures, with the door facing away. This is the womens' menstrual hut and is used by the women each month, for it is the belief that at such times a magic power descends on women. This power makes them dangerous to everyone around them, but especially to men and the tools men use. If they touch the man's hunting equipment, it will not work, and if they eat the game a man kills, the meat will be poisoned.

It is strange that beliefs such as these are still present in the twentieth century, but, although dying out with the more modern Pima, the taboo is very evident in remote villages, especially among the older people.

The Pima, like the Papago, are a patriarchal and patrilineal society and are separated into patrilineal clans. These clans are composed of a man and all his descendants through his sons. Women belong to the clan of their father, but when they marry, their children go with the father's, not the mother's clan. This makes it extremely important for a man to have sons in order to perpetuate the clan.

There are four clans in the Pima Tribe, some say five, but the fifth is not very distinct. The names of these cannot be accurately translated into English, but they are Apap, Apki, Mam, Vaf, and Okari. Even though the clan regulates marriages and other activities, the village is the center of Pima life.

Most of the people in a village are related, generally on the father's side and each village selects a headman who is a sort of judge and leader in many activities. He settles quarrels and decides the time and place for ceremonies. His home is the meeting house where community, social, and political gatherings are held.

It is the responsibility of the headman to keep the sacred things that belong to the village. It may be a string of eagle feathers which can produce rain, or perhaps a magic stone or a carved image. These sacred objects are placed in a large square basket and kept in the headman's home or hidden in a safe place in the desert known only to him. He must know the magic speeches which are recited to bring rain or to chase away disease, and he presides at all ceremonies. Before the headman dies, he chooses one of his young relatives as his replacement. He teaches him all the secret and magic operations of his office so village life continues uninterrupted at his death.

These activities are carried on in the remote, isolated villages but in the centers of population where whites have "modernized" the Pima, the old customs are dying out. The Pima and the Maricopa were both peaceful and industrious. They welcomed the Spaniards and immediately, acculturation began. However, it was not until the arrival of the Americans in Arizona that rapid erosion of their culture began. The tribe prospered economically as they supplied travelers, settlers, U. S. Army units, and gold seekers with grain and livestock.

Unfortunately, many of the people the Pima met were not the cream of American society and they were poorly treated by those who ventured into Pimeria. Murderers, outlaws, rough army men and land-hungry (and water-hungry) settlers brought them immeasurable suffering and degradation. Outlaws killed and plundered and settlers took land and water. Although the tribes grew much grain and utilized the finest agricultural methods, this prosperity came to an end when the water of the Gila River was dammed up and diverted from the reservation fields to white-owned farms and ranches shortly before 1900. The crops of the Maricopa and Pima withered and their fields returned to desert. This caused them to decline to abject poverty. At one time, it was proposed that the Pima and Maricopa be moved to Oklahoma. This would have been a death sentence for many of the people, for they would have succumbed to the severe winter cold or the stifling summer humidity.

The homeland of the Pima and Maricopa tribes was in Mexico until 1853, when jurisdiction was transferred to the United States by Mexico via the Gadsen Purchase. A 64,000-acre reservation was established for the Indians in 1859, but the Pima leaders felt it was too small.  Finally, after ten years of political maneuvering, the reservation was increased by 81,000 acres to give the tribes 145,000 acres of land.  The main area of trust land is the Gila River Indian Reservation with headquarters at Sacaton, Arizona.  However, a number of Pima make their homes on smaller reservations such as Maricopa Indian Reservation and Salt River Indian Reservation.  In 1921 about one fourth of the Gila River Reservation was allotted to individual Indian families.  Since then, because of division among family members as allottees die, these parcels have been broken up into worthless, tiny segments of land.

Before the appearance of white settlers in their areas, the Pima had plenty of water and used the irrigation canals developed by their ancestors, the Hohokam.  Thus, they were always assured of a bountiful harvest.  As more and more whites made their homes along the Gila River, they depleted the water supply, leaving little for Indian use.  The United States built Coolidge Dam in the 1920s to relieve the situation by providing control and storage of the water, but this did not help the Pima.  The water then, just as it is now, was diverted away from Indian farms and toward white agricultural land.

The irony of this entire condition manifests itself in the federal Indian policy.  Since the beginning of the United States, it has been the goal to turn Indians into farmers, while the Pima, who had been excellent farmers for centuries, were so inadequately protected that they were unable to follow their traditional ways.  Even today much of the land which does produce abundant agricultural products is under long-term lease, at low rates to non-Indians.  These "short-change" leases have been negotiated by the great protector of Indian rights, the Bureau of Indian Affairs.

Established in 1824 by President James Monroe as the guardian of the rights of Indians, the over 150-year history of the Bureau indicates a totally inefficient, paternalistic operation which falls far short of President Monroe's intent.  Their philosophy reveals more exploitation than advocacy in the treatment of most of America's native people.  Because of the location of the Pima's

Gila River Reservation, between the ever-growing Phoenix and the rapidly expanding Tucson, the wasteland of the desert has become the "Golden Corridor," some of the most valuable land in the state.  The Salt River Reservation, likewise an unwanted area for years, lies adjacent to the cities of Mesa, Tempe, and Scottsdale, and is now prime land for the expansion of these suburban giants which are bulging at the seams with population growth.  Unless the tribes can protect their reservation borders and unless the BIA can change its ineffective policy of land retention, these pockets of Indians will be eroded until there will be no land left for the River People.

Residents of the reservations now engage in a variety of on- and off-reservation activities which include many forms of agriculture such as crop farming and cattle raising, as well as industrial ventures in diamond cutting and polishing, processing sugar beets, computer card key punching, and the marketing of native handicrafts.

On the freeway between Phoenix and Tucson is the Gila River Arts and Crafts Center which provides an outlet for the famous Pima baskets and other Indian manufactured items from all over the United States.  An Indian-operated restaurant is located in the same complex and, like the Crafts Center, does a thriving business selling Indian articles, specifically frybread, chili, and other delicious southwestern culinary masterpieces.

Another tourist attraction and facility used by many sportsmen from the local area is Firebird Lake Water Sports World. This development is one of the most enterprising recreational endeavors of any Indian tribe.  A marina provides residents of the Valley of the Sun with the opportunity to go boating, water-skiing, swimming, or to picnic at the lake shore only minutes from their homes.  Special aquatic attractions are scheduled throughout the year and Firebird Lake, with its own restaurant, concessions, and other functional facilities has become a nationally known recreational area.

These installations, in addition to other tribal business ventures such as three industrial parks at Chandler, Coolidge, and San Tan have started the Pima and Maricopa at Gila River

Reservation on the road to economic improvement. The Salt River Reservation has also become actively engaged in changing their economic status by developing similar projects.

Slowly but surely, the Pima and Maricopa Indians are learning the art of living in two worlds, and in doing so, are providing a more stable economic base for their tribal members without compromising their cultural integrity. By drawing the best from the dominant society's technological advances, and combining these facets with the spiritual and aesthetic qualities of traditional cultural concepts, these two tribal groups have synthesized a way of life which may preserve them from oblivion.

# 4
# Colorado River Tribes

Scattered along the lower Colorado River from Hoover Dam to the point where it empties into the Gulf of California are several groups of agriculture-based Indians. Unlike the peaceful Papago and Pima, these tribes are quite fierce and warlike and tolerated little aggression from alien Europeans, and later Americans, without retaliation.

First contacted by Hernando de Alarcon in 1540, who intended to bring supplies up the Colorado River to replenish the Coronado expedition, the Yuma people were always very volatile. Juan de Oñate and his entourage were the next whites to visit the area in 1605 and, since the Spaniards were merely passing through, there was no controversy and the meeting was peaceful. In 1701 and 1702, Father Eusebio Kino made two visits to the Colorado River tribes and established friendly relations as was his practice. He did not attempt any permanent mission activities and the atmosphere remained calm and amiable. It was not until 1774–75 that Juan Bautista de Anza and Father Francisco Garces established two permanent missions along the

Colorado. These two efforts attempted to emulate the successful missionizing of the Southern California Indians, but it was
soon found that the tactics used in California were not appropriate for these "warriors."

Garces and de Anza built two churches and began the conver-
sion of the Indians in typical Spanish-Jesuit manner. Their
ecclesiastical activity was heavily supported by Spanish military
might which had established a horrendous reputation in dealing
with Indians. It took only two years for the natives to rebel
against the attempts at Christianization. In July, 1781, the
Yuma killed every white in their territory and destroyed the
mission churches. Because the Indians were so ferocious in
their attack and so adamant against the encroachment into
their religious institutions, Spanish mission endeavors were
never again attempted.

True to the Spanish method of dealing with Indians, a puni-
tive expedition was sent against the Yuma, but it had very little
success and Spain abandoned any further action in the Lower
Colorado area.

The tribal units which inhabit the region, the Yuman-speaking
Yuma or Quechan, the Mojave and the Cocopa, and the Sho-
shonean-speaking Chemehuevi are much alike in their culture,
but quite different from most other southwestern Indians. As
noted earlier, the Yuma are rather aggressive in nature. This
does not follow the characteristics of most southwestern agricultural Indians. These descendants of the Patayan culture are
also much larger in size than most of their neighbors, many of
the men exceeding six feet in height.

## CHEMEHUEVI

The Chemehuevi, besides speaking a Shoshonean dialect, also
are much smaller in height than the Yuma. It is generally
thought that they are offshoots from the Paiute tribes. They
were semiagricultural, raising crops such as corn, squash, and
beans, but not to the same degree as most of their neighbors.
Living simple lives, they survived primarily by hunting small

game, fishing, and gathering roots and seeds which grew in their territory. Being smaller than other Colorado River people, the Chemehuevi were not as strong physically. They did not utilize canoes but used rafts made of reeds to travel on the river and catch fish.

Clothing was sparse, consisting of breechcloths for the men, if they wore anything at all, and skirts or aprons woven of willow bark for the women. Their hair was the center of much attention and was worn quite long. Many hours were spent in brushing and grooming it. Other cosmetic attention was directed toward tattooing which was considered necessary to allow one to enter the land of the dead. The nasal septum was pierced so pendants could be attached and earrings were worn by both sexes.

The tribe was never considered to be warlike even though they did participate in hostilities with some of their neighbors. More often, being rather timid and nonaggressive, they were less involved in open warfare and were inclined to utilize political alliances with other passive tribes.

Having originally lived in the Great Basin area of Nevada, Utah, and northwestern Arizona, the Chemehuevi slowly drifted southward until, by the mid-1800s, most were living along the Colorado River where they were greatly influenced by their neighbors, especially the Mojave.

A small reservation was established for one band of Chemehuevi at Twenty Nine Palms, California, but by 1909 most of the members had moved to Banning, California to work in the fruit orchards and had taken up residence on the Morongo Reservation with the Cahuilla or in the city of Indio. By 1913, the reservation was abandoned.

In 1907, the Chemehuevi Valley Reservation was established on the California side of the Colorado River near present-day Lake Havasu City. However, when the Parker Dam was completed in 1938, the waters of Lake Havasu inundated their lands and most of the tribal members moved to the Colorado River Indian Reservation, where they live today.

The Chemehuevi earned the reputation of being excellent weavers of baskets which were similar to the products of their

Paiute cousins. Recent popularity of Indian arts and crafts has brought on increasing demands and caused a change in craftsmanship. The older styles of coiled and twined basketry have been replaced with a highly developed open style of finely woven, coiled basketry. Using native plants, the Chemehuevi created exquisite trays, bowls, and jars with striking geometric and life-form designs. The original basketry style has nearly disappeared, and by 1978, only two Chemehuevi women and one man maintained the custom. These three artisans produce traditional basketry of excellent quality that is highly prized by collectors.

## MOJAVE

The largest and most warlike of the Indian tribes of the Colorado River area was the Mojave. There were 3000 to 4000 of these aggressive people in prewhite times which made them a power in the Southwest. They utilized traditional bows and arrows in frequent battles with their neighbors, but their favorite weapon was a war club made of mesquite or ironwood.

Personal appearance was important to both sexes and much time was devoted to care of the hair and face. They wore their hair quite long with bangs in the front. It was glossy black from shampooing and conditioning using mesquite gum mixtures. Their faces were ornately decorated with red, white, and black paint, and tattoos on the chin identified a person according to clan affiliation. Ornaments of shell were popular, and both men and women wore shell earrings.

The Mojaves have always been farmers and for centuries have cultivated the fertile river bottom land in the Mojave Valley. Utilizing floodwater from the Colorado to grow corn, squash, beans, sunflowers, tobacco, and other domesticated crops, they supplemented their diets by hunting and gathering.

Being great travelers, the Mojave journeyed down the Colorado to visit and trade with their allies, the Yuma. They also regularly crossed the desert to the west, traveling clear to the Pacific Ocean to trade with the Chumash Indians around present-day

Santa Barbara, California. These expeditions were made on foot, and distances of nearly one hundred miles could be covered in one day by the men traveling at a steady, even trot. They could go without food for at least four days, using a doughlike mixture from which they sucked liquid and which also provided some sustenance.

Although they were quite warlike, the Mojave presented little interference to American westward expansion. There were some skirmishes and a few killings, but the activity was minimal when compared to the other southwestern fighting tribes.

The traditional religious belief of the Mojave was that all power came from one deity called Mastamho. He created the Colorado River, made light come to the earth, shaped the land with hills and valleys, and created the people who inhabited it. The paramount religious activities were the ceremonies associated with death and disposition of the dead. They practiced no inhumation and restricted their funerary arrangements to cremation. They were affected strongly by dreams and felt supernatural power was acquired in this manner.

Fort Mohave[14] was completed in 1859 in the Mohave Valley near Needles, California and the area surrounding it was designated as a reservation in 1880. The Colorado River Indian Reservation was established in 1865 encompassing nearly 226,000 acres. These two trust areas are the homelands for most of the Mojave people today.

Encouraged by the federal government, the people began practicing agriculture to a greater degree, and in 1867 they dug the first irrigation canal with shovels, removing the earth in baskets. This was their introduction to the white man's modern farming techniques and, although they had many problems during the transition period, the Mojave are now confirmed agriculturists.

Their arts and crafts do not provide a great amount of income for, although they have always done some basket weaving and pottery making, most of these crafts were utilitarian and not made to sell. Around the turn of the twentieth century some unique ceramic figurines, dressed in replicas of traditional clothing, were produced for the tourist trade. Today, however, very few of these are seen and pottery of any kind is scarce. The only other crafts produced are articles of beadwork in the form of capes or collars and, occasionally, some "finger woven" or braided cradleboard straps.

The 268,691-acre Colorado River Indian Reservation is now the home for nearly 1800 Mojave, Chemehuevi, Hopi, and Navajo Indians. The inhabitants, although culturally diverse, make every attempt to preserve their cultural heritage. They have built a museum and library at the tribal headquarters near Parker, Arizona. There, information concerning the tribes and their history is available, and many examples of traditional basketry and pottery from the past are on display. Visitors can also purchase the limited Mojave beadwork and pottery, silver ornamentations by both Navajo and Hopi artisans, Chemehuevi baskets, and other arts and crafts produced by the four tribes in residence on the reservation.

Income from these facilities is sizable and supplements the tribal resources obtained from other endeavors. There is a Senior Citizens' Clock Factory which not only provides income for the tribes through the sale of clocks, but is a source of gainful employment for elderly Indians. Along the Colorado River, marinas have been built which provide recreational activities for tourists and, because of the climate and plentiful water, they have proven quite lucrative ventures for the tribes. The most profitable endeavors, though, are in the areas of agriculture. There are more than 70,000 acres under cultivation on the reservation with a gross income of more than $52 million. Some of the irrigated fields of alfalfa, cotton, grains, and vegetables are operated by tribal members, but many are under long-term leases to non-Indians.

During World War II, about 20,000 Japanese-Americans were incarcerated in concentration camps built on the Colorado River Indian Reservation. After the conflict ended, the prisoners were allowed to return to their West Coast homes, and the camps were no longer needed. Many of the facilities were turned over to the tribes and some are still in use.

As indicated, the Mojave people and the other three tribes living on this parcel of trust land have fared well economically.

The acculturation process and monetary stability has not been easily acquired or without a large price tag. To attain this status, the Indians have had to sacrifice a part of the traditional culture and take on a portion of the dominant society's value system. Who is to say if the price is too high?

## QUECHAN

Downriver from the Colorado River Indian Reservation is the land of the Quechan (Yuma) Indians. When the Spanish reached the area in the sixteenth century, they called the people "Yuma," which means "the son of the leader." Evidently, one Quechan, as they call themselves, introduced himself as "Yuma" and the Spanish assumed this was the name of the entire group.

The Quechan culture and history has been similar to the other Yuman tribes which inhabited the Colorado River Valley. Houses were simple, made of poles and brush and the principal means of subsistance was agriculture, supplemented by wild vegetable gathering, hunting, and fishing. They practiced cremation of the dead and placed great importance on dreams, which were considered to be spiritual experiences.

Except for the disastrous results of the Christian-Quechan experience related earlier, most of the Spanish encounters were on a friendly basis. They were not so friendly with their neighbors, however, and drove the Maricopa completely out of their homeland, the victims taking refuge with the Pima.[15] Sporadically, the Quechan were at odds with every tribe in the area, being on good terms occasionally with the Kamia from Southern California and the Mojave from upstream.

By the 1850s, gold seekers, utilizing the southern route to California, began the first sizable influx of whites into Yuma territory since the Spanish gave up on their colonization. Steamboats began to appear on the Colorado River and in 1853, Fort Yuma was built near the site of the destroyed Jesuit missions. In 1883, the Fort Yuma Indian Reservation was established to include 48,000 acres of land. Later, the reservation was reduced drastically until there are less than 10,000 acres left today. Most of the land retained by the Quechan is located in Imperial County, California, but a small portion of land and tribal headquarters are in Arizona.

Having an original population of 3000 or 4000, the Quechan now have less than 1800 members, of which less than half live on the reservation. This small group, however, has been quite progressive and has nearly 7000 acres of land under irrigation. They have also developed a trailer park and a construction company which adds revenue to the tribal treasury. Recreation activities on the Colorado River also provide economic stimulus.

The Quechan, like the other Colorado River tribes mentioned earlier, have paid a price for this acculturation. Most signs of traditional Quechan culture have disappeared and the people are much like their white counterparts in cultural practice. A few women still produce some beadwork, and a few other craft items are made in limited quantities, but they do not play an important part in the total economic picture of the Quechan people.

## COCOPAH

Another group of Yuman-speaking Indians living along the Colorado River are the Cocopah. Originally from Baja California, a part of this tribe has lived around the mouth of the Colorado since before the coming of the first white men to the area in 1540. Most of their relatives still reside in Mexico, however, and only a few live in Arizona. Basically an agricultural people, their culture was similar to that of the Quechan and other neighboring tribes. The Cocopah were probably the most peaceful of all the Yuman groups although they would battle fiercely if their homes and families were threatened. Generally, they did not enter into any warfare with whites or other Indians without strong provocation.

The Cocopah were not highly skilled in the arts and crafts, and most of their products were strictly utilitarian. They made some pottery and baskets but never developed their skills to the point where their products were marketable. They did make shell beads and other adornments and decorated their faces with ornate painting.

By the mid-1800s, the Cocopah began to be exposed to large numbers of whites, as were their Quechan neighbors. Gold seekers, river boats, and Anglo farmers began to effect changes in the Cocopah way of life. The water from the Colorado River was channeled off for irrigating non-Indian farmland and this left the water supply for the tribe insufficient for their traditional farming methods, as well as deficient in sustaining an adequate amount of wild foods along the shore. This led to economic and cultural deprivation and a loss of traditional life-styles.

For many years the Cocopah merely existed with poor housing, abject poverty, and severe educational retardation which prevented them from ameliorating their problems. It was not until the 1970s that things began to change for them. Housing development was started, agricultural land was irrigated and improved, and the Cocopah youth became involved with modern education. In 1978, 13 young people from the tribal population of about 465 were attending colleges and universities.

Because of the severe cultural erosion, very little income is derived from crafts. A few women market some beadwork and make colorful rag dolls, but the principal source of income is from off-reservation employment for meager wages. The tribal members supplement these small paychecks by raising vegetables for home consumption.

As we have seen, the Colorado River Indians have suffered a great amount economically and culturally because of their exposure to the dominant society. Because control of the most precious commodity in the West, water, is generally in the hands of non-Indians, these tribes, which historically have been farmers, have had to endure assimilation into a new way of life to obtain economic survival. Consequently, the loss of cultural practices has led to a situation of "cultural genocide" and an eradication of a way of life for entire nations of Indian people.

# 5
# The Pai People

Living on the northern and western plateaus of the State of Arizona are three tribes of Indians called the Pai People, the Hualapai, the Yavapai, and the Havasupai. The Paiute are also included with this group, although they are from a different cultural and linguistic background. The first three groups speak dialects of the Yuman language, as do the tribes discussed in the previous chapter, the Quechan, the Mojave, and the Cocopah, while the Paiute speak a dialect of the Shoshonean language. The Pai People are characterized by a simple way of life and an uncomplicated social structure reflecting intense individualism. Their society places a heavy emphasis on family self-sufficiency, and there is an absence of elaborate formal tribal organization. Of the four tribes, only the Havasupai have traditionally been farmers, with the Hualapai, Yavapai, and Paiute gaining their subsistence primarily by hunting and gathering.

## HAVASUPAI

The Havasupai live in one of the most beautiful spots on earth, Cataract Canyon, a side branch of Grand Canyon. The name of the tribe means "people of the blue water," so called because of the blue-green water which flows through their homeland. The tribe uses this water to irrigate their crops of corn, beans, and squash. The Havasupai were not farmers originally, but they learned how to irrigate and raise vegetables from the Hopi centuries ago. They also copied their pueblo style of living from these neighbors and even incorporated many facets of pueblo culture in their everyday life-style. This means the tribe had permanent residences and were not a nomadic group as were their relatives the Hualapai and the Yavapai. They sometimes even utilized caves for homes as they carried on their peaceful ways.

Securely nestled deep in their sanctuary, the Havasupai did not get caught up in the "Indian Wars" of the last half of the nineteenth century. This helped them in maintaining their culture unchanged, for there was little contact with the outside world and, consequently, little pressure from the dominant society to acculturate. Cataract Canyon, along with surrounding areas of land, was established as the Havasupai Indian Reservation on June 8, 1880. It contained only 3,055 acres until 1975, when the reservation was enlarged by adding 48,000 acres to it. At the same time, the United States gave the tribe the right to use another 137,000 acres of surrounding plateau land.

The people have raised cattle very successfully for a number of years, and their farms on the floor of the canyon produce peaches, nectarines, apricots, and figs in addition to vegetables. Nuts and mesquite beans are harvested in the late fall for a dietary supplement.

Arts and crafts do not play an important role in their economy, but some basketry is practiced along with pottery making learned from the Hopi. Agriculture and tourism provides most of the tribal income. Because of their isolation and the beauty of their area, the Havasupai have developed a profitable tourist business.

Since they are located in such an inaccessible place, the Havasupai have been able to capitalize on and control the visitors. Only one trail leads into this "Shangri La" and unless tourists fly in by helicopter, they must utilize the trail and are required to carry all their refuse out of the canyon when they leave. This prevents spoiling the beauty of the canyon by turning it into a gigantic garbage can.

## HUALAPAI

The Hualapai, "Pine Tree People," live south of the lower Grand Canyon, north and east of Kingman, Arizona. Before 1875, they lived with the Mojave but, because of friction between the tribes, the Hualapai moved. After attempts by the government to relocate them back on the Colorado River Indian Reservation failed to budge them, the present reservation was established.

These Yuman-speaking people are traditionally hunters and gatherers and only farm to supplement their diets. Because of the diversity of the land, with elevations varying from 1200 to 7400 feet, the Hualapai are able to find a wide variety of foods, both animal and vegetable. Mescal, a cactus which has narcotic effects when used, is a staple item in the diets of the tribespeople.

The Hualapai were first contacted by the Spanish about 1598, and they were friendly with the whites for a good while. After some of their leaders were killed though, they took up arms. Finally defeated by the United States Army, they were moved back to the reservation.

Tourism has proven to be the tribe's most lucrative endeavor and is growing each year. Attractions include the Hualapai Arts and Crafts Center and the Tribal Culture Center. Visitors can go hunting, fishing, hiking, and camping and take a wild two-day raft trip down the Colorado River.

The Hualapai Reservation has the only access into the inner gorge of the Grand Canyon by car. Fees are charged by the tribe for use of roads or other facilities and these add to a small tribal treasury. The roads are not well developed and it is a complicated process to keep from getting lost, so this drive over twenty-two miles of bumpy, gravel roads is not undertaken by large numbers of tourists.

Although Hualapai income is derived from various sources, the tribe is extremely poor. Poverty has plagued them for a long time and presents a critical issue to the tribal council. Being a conservative tribe and not wanting to open their homeland totally to outside people, which would hasten the erosion of their culture, the Hualapai have closed the entire western portion of the reservation and made it off limits to all tourists. This act sacrifices economic development but promotes the retention of Hualapai cultural traditions. The Hualapai are not yet ready to pay the awesome price for economic stability. Decisions on issues such as these are facing a majority of the Indian nations today.

## YAVAPAI

The third group of Pai People are the Yavapai whose traditional homeland was in central Arizona, especially around present-day Prescott. They hunted and gathered food, built temporary houses of poles, brush, and adobe for summer use and lived in caves during the winter months. They spoke the Yuman language and much of their culture was similar to that of their northern relatives, the Hualapai and the Havasupai, which we discussed earlier. Because of their close contact with the Apache bands, the Yavapai adopted many traits of these neighbors and were often mistakenly identified as Apache. Even today they are sometimes referred to as Yavapai-Apache or sometimes by the equally incorrect name of Mojave-Apache.

Early white contact was minimal, and it was not until the mid-1800s that the Yavapai began to suffer from white encroachments. The Yavapai responded with raids and war parties closely resembling those of the Apache and, in fact, sometimes the Apache joined the Yavapai as allies, which also contributed to the mistaken identity.

During the 1860s and 1870s the Yavapai were moved around Arizona on several reservations. Finally, in 1873, they were placed on the San Carlos Apache Reservation where they stayed for twenty-five years. Around the turn of the twentieth century, they began to leave San Carlos and return to their homeland. Today the Yavapai reside primarily on three reservations located in central Arizona.

The first, Fort McDowell Reservation, was established in 1903 along the desert foothills on the Verde River near its confluence with the Salt River, just east of Scottsdale. The reservation consists of 24,680 acres of low desert hills and tree-lined river bottom land. Some 350 residents engage in farming and cattle raising on a very limited basis, gravel mining, and some woodcutting. Most income for the tribal members, however, comes from hourly wage occupations off-reservation. Some money comes to the tribe from recreational activities and from leases to the City of Phoenix for water pumping and filtration stations located on tribal land along the rivers.

It was thought by many that tribalism was dead at Fort McDowell, but in 1968, the people dispelled such thoughts. That year, the federal government passed the Central Arizona Enabling Act designed to increase the state's water resources. One portion of the act provided for the construction of Orme Dam which, although it would have provided water needed for the thirsty state, would have inundated the Fort McDowell Reservation. Naturally, the Yavapai objected vigorously to this action. Enlisting the aid of environmentalists and other interested citizens, the Yavapai were able to stop the work on the dam, and eventually the government set aside plans for the entire project, temporarily at least. The Yavapai were more interested in retaining their land, the very core of their religious life, than they were in receiving a few dollars which would soon be gone.

A little beadwork is being done at Fort McDowell and, although their culture is being threatened, the Yavapai are taking steps to perpetuate it. Library collections of artifacts and cultural documents are being developed in the new tribal headquarters building. Some of the exquisite Yavapai baskets, which rival even the Apache baskets, are being made, and a small amount of weaving is also found on the reservation.

World's tallest fountain taking water from the thirsty desert adjacent to Fort McDowell Reservation.

Up the Verde River at the site of historic Fort Verde is another reservation of Yavapai Indians. The 635 acres of trust land which comprises Camp Verde Reservation, is divided into several plots of ground. It was designated a reservation as the result of land purchases by the government in 1914 and 1916. Portions of real estate have also been acquired from individuals and corporations and added to the reservation in more recent times. An example is the Clarkdale Indian Community, a modern subdivision of 40 three-, four- and five-bedroom homes in the town of Clarkdale. This sixty-acre plot was occupied by a number of Indian people who worked in mines operated by Phelps-Dodge Mining Company. When the copper-mining operation closed in the 1950s, the company gave the land to the tribe and it was included in the reservation. The entire reservation is still quite small and, for the most part, not developed except for farming.

Most employment for the tribal members consists of operating the ranches and farms along the Verde River and some are production workers in a small garment factory in Cottonwood. A few are employed by the tribe, and the National Park Service has seasonal jobs at the famous Indian ruins in the area (Montezuma's Well, Montezuma's Castle, and Tuzigoot National Monument). A tribal cultural center is currently under construction at the entrance to Montezuma's Castle National Monument. It is scheduled to open in the early 1980s. This will provide a cultural resurgence for the people as well as an outlet for the beadwork and basketry made by the women of the Camp Verde Reservation.

The third reservation for the Yavapai is located in the city of Prescott. It was officially designated as the Yavapai-Prescott Indian Reservation in 1935, primarily because the citizens of the city donated land and championed the cause of the Indians. The small seventy-five-acre portion of land formerly assigned to Fort Whipple was expanded in the 1950s to 1409 acres.

Today, the tribe is utilizing the proximity of the rapidly growing city of Prescott by developing an industrial park and leasing frontage property to local businesses. Soon the tribe plans to build a modern shopping center and intends to enter the construction industry.

Reservation homes are modern and have all the conveniences and utilities of any other part of Prescott. The children of the sixty-eight tribal members who live there attend public schools in the town. A growing interest in higher education has been demonstrated and several of the youth are attending Yavapai Community College located near the reservation, or other more distant colleges and universities.

Like most Indian tribes, the Yavapai are attempting to make the most of their limited size and small resources to develop functional economic units which will enable those Indians who wish to do so, the prerogative of living in their homeland. They have reestablished their tribalism and are progressing in the modern world without sacrificing the value systems and traditions which have enabled them to survive as Indians.

## PAIUTE

In the Great Basin area of the southwestern United States live the Paiute Indians. They are probable descendants of the very ancient Basket Maker Indians of the plateau, for they have closely related traits. Their traditional housing is somewhat similar, excellent coiled basketry is made, and the economic structure is quite like that of the earlier group.

The largest permanent residential unit for these people has always been the family. Although special occasions, such as the rabbit hunt, may have temporarily brought larger numbers together, most of the time there was little evidence of the extended family as found in other tribal societies. The nuclear families wandered about during the summer months seeking the elements necessary for daily survival and grouped together in small village units of two to ten families for a more communal life in the winter. Game drives took place during this time and occasionally there would be enough leisure time for a little community interaction in the form of singing and dancing. Each family maintained its autonomy in these loose village structures though, and just as each family might realign itself with different villages, the villages might join an entirely new group of villages for the occasional game drive. There was little political organization of a permanent nature.

Because of this lack of political organization, the Paiute lacked definite warfare. Violence, raids, and feuds were evident but were carried on without any special regalia or ritual. Generally, these skirmishes were between speakers of different languages and were most frequently motivated by woman-stealing. After the introduction of the horse by the Spaniards, horse-stealing became the most prevalent cause for fighting.

Basically, the Paiute are divided into two dialectic groupings. The Northern Paiute, along with the Bannock, constitute one dialectic portion of the Shoshonean Branch of the Uto-Aztecan linguistic family. In prewhite times, their homeland covered western Nevada, southeastern Oregon, and a strip of California east of the Sierra Nevadas as far south as Owens Lake. Most of this territory falls outside the boundaries established for this manuscript, so the attention of this section will focus on the Southern Paiute bands.

This division belongs to the Ute-Chemehuevi element of the Shoshonean branch of the Uto-Aztecan language family. These bands inhabit western Utah, northwestern Arizona, southeastern Nevada, and parts of southeastern California. The population of these scattered bands has been almost impossible to ascertain and, even today, there is no accurate count. A loose estimation of 3000 to 4000 might be representative of today's Paiute, including both major units of the tribe. Although there have been numerous Paiute and they have been involved in many activities connected with "settling the West," extensive research has not been in evidence. The name Paiute has become identified with "Digger Indians" and has been assigned a rather contemptuous connotation, thereby erasing some of the romantic attention accorded other tribes in America. Although their material wealth was never great and they had to work hard to survive in the forbidding desert environment, the Paiute utilized their resources to the fullest and lived comparatively happy lives.

In 1847 an event took place which would have a drastic effect
on the lives of the Paiute people. It was in that year that
Brigham Young led his band of "Mormons" into the Salt Lake
Valley in Utah.[16] Attempting to establish a theocracy called
"Deseret," Young incurred the wrath of the United States
government, which dispatched troops to Utah to bring the
Mormons under federal control. The expedition never entered
into armed fighting and Young yielded his office as President
of Deseret to an American governor of the Utah Territory.
Feelings ran high, however, for quite some time and the Mormons, who had established friendly relations with the Paiute,
found ready allies for any military or vigilante activity.

One incident, the Mountain Meadows Massacre, illustrates
the potent military force which was available by combining
the Mormon and Paiute warriors.

As the U.S. Army approached Deseret, the inhabitants were
quite angry, and a California-bound wagon train also moved into
the territory. This ordinarily would not have caused concern, but
the men of the immigrating party openly boasted of having a part
in driving the Mormons out of Missouri and Illinois. They also
taunted the settlers concerning their fate when the military
arrived. When the group reached Mountain Meadows in southern
Utah, the 140 men, women, and children were attacked by the
Mormon-Paiute force and all were killed except for 18 children
thought to be too young to give evidence against the attackers.

Brigham Young was incensed by what had happened and
issued strict orders which prevented a recurrence of this type of
action by his followers. The Mormons found, however, that it
was much easier to incite the Indians to violence than it was to
calm them, and the Paiute continued for some time to harass
pioneers crossing their territory. The situation was finally
brought under control on January 29, 1863, when a contingent
of California and Nevada volunteers under the command of
Brigadier General Patrick E. Connor defeated the combined
Shoshone and Paiute forces at Bear River. This brought peace
to the area and the Indians agreed to permit travel on the
trails and the construction of a railroad.

Aside from the involvement with the Mormons, the Paiute association with encroaching European cultures was rather casual. Consequently, they were able to stay in the vicinity of their homeland on the north rim of the Grand Canyon in the area along the Arizona-Utah border. The largest population center which will be discussed as typical of the Paiute community is the Kaibab Paiute Indian Reservation. This trust land is the most remote from Arizona's metropolitan areas and is not on the "tourist trail." The people have been fairly isolated and not subjected to the same cultural erosion as Indians in other portions of the Southwest. Acculturation is evident in many facets of Paiute life, but it has been brought about in a more subtle manner and more voluntarily than with most tribes.

The Kaibab Paiute made very little pottery, but in the past were excellent basket weavers, producing a wide variety of baskets. This included large conical baskets, parching and winnowing basket trays, pitch-covered water jars, basketry caps, and semibasketry cradles. Today, the Kaibab weave very little for utilitarian use and, since tourism is not a great facet in their economic structure, they do not manufacture a large amount for sale.

The only visitor attraction of any note which contributes to the tribal treasury is the famous Pipe Spring National Monument. This fort, built in 1870 by Mormons to protect settlers from Indian attacks, attracts a number of tourists each year, some of whom also purchase arts and crafts from the Paiute.

Of a total enrollment of 195 Kaibab Paiute, only 110 were living on the reservation in 1978. The lack of employment opportunities on this remote reservation forces many to move away to find work. Some do make a living by raising cattle, farming small plots of land, or working in nearby lumbering operations. Several thousand acres of grazing land are leased each year to non-Indian cattlemen.

These meager additions to tribal income do not make the Kaibab Paiute wealthy. The slow development of interest in industrial and commercial enterprises would indicate that these

Indians may be more interested in maintaining their peace and privacy than in entering the "rat race" of the dominant society. With the beauty of the mountains and canyons, the grandeur of the vermillion cliffs nearby, they have aesthetic attractions which they value much more than the material acquisitions of the outside world.

# 6
# Apache

Apache!  No other Indian group in North America is better known to the general public than the Apache.  Likewise, no other group of Indians in America have been as denigrated and misunderstood as these comparative newcomers to the Southwest.  Although most people have heard of the Apache, few have heard the truth and even fewer actually have more than a cursory concept of Apache values or lifeways.  Most accept presentations in the media and cheap novels of barbarous, murdering, cruel savages as adequate descriptions of a highly honorable, brave, and trustworthy people.  In this section, the author will attempt a valid, objective presentation of the Apache as they struggled for survival in the midst of a hostile environment surrounded by even more hostile neighbors.

The Apache are linguistically related to the native Indians in the interior of Alaska and the Yukon Territory of Canada. Arriving in this hemisphere, according to archaeologists, two or three thousand years ago from Asia, the Athapaskan began to move slowly south and east.  They were seeking new hunting grounds and, at the same time, relieving the congestion caused by the arrival of new waves of people across the Bering Strait.

The route which eventually led these nomadic groups to the Southwest is fairly well agreed upon. They traveled down the Pacific Coast and inland valleys along narrow corridors until they reached the present-day Washington-Oregon area. They then crossed the Cascades; and their route took them along the eastern slopes of the Rocky Mountains and to the Southern Plains area of Kansas, Oklahoma, Texas, and New Mexico. As they moved along this trail, small bands split off and went their own way. This accounts for the fragmented sections of Athapaskan-speaking peoples in the Northwest and along the Pacific Coast in California.[17] After contacts with some of the warriors of the Plains, most of the Apache groups gradually moved westward into the mountainous areas where the Spaniards found them in the early sixteenth century. By the middle of the nineteenth century, as the result of pressure from various Indian groups combined with force applied by the Mexicans and Americans, the Apache were compressed into the areas they inhabited during the "Apache Wars," which were primarily a desperate struggle by these resolute people to escape annihilation.

The Kiowa-Apache and the Lipan had established a precarious foothold and lived on the Plains. The Jicarilla Apache ranged over the mountainous area of northeastern New Mexico and southeastern Colorado. The Mescalero occupied territory in south-central New Mexico, western Texas, and northern Mexico. The Chiricahua were located in southeastern Arizona, southwestern New Mexico, and northern Mexico. The final group, the Western Apache, inhabited the White Mountains of eastern Arizona. The Navajo, another branch of Apacheans, will be discussed in a later chapter.

These mountainous homes not only provided the Apache with excellent hunting grounds and fertile valley land to raise corn, beans, and squash, but they also protected them from the enemies who were so plentiful. The Spanish had much to do with changing the Apache from a comparatively friendly group who lived in relative harmony with their neighbors to the "enemy" as their name connotes in the Zuni language. Since the Spanish could not conquer these fiercely independent fighters, they began the tactic of agitation between the tribes. This proved very successful, for it was not long until the Apache were considered a renegade people by almost everyone. The ancient military philosophy which is still in use very successfully today, "divide and conquer," was utilized to the fullest by the Spanish, the Mexican, and the Americans in their dealings with the Apache. The efforts to exterminate the tribe were herculean, even involving voluntary alliances among the Indians as well as with the whites.

None of these activities, as damaging as they were, could wipe out the extremely cunning and ferocious Apache. Bounties were paid for their scalps, captives were enslaved, and gigantic military campaigns were launched against them, but still the Apache persisted and survived. They simply refused to be exterminated or to surrender.

Throughout the nineteenth century, the Apache defended their homeland and kept the invading forces always on the defensive. Nothing seemed to quench the indomitable courage with which these small groups fought for their homes and freedom. It was not until 1886, after over two years of seige that the "Apache Wars" were concluded with the surrender of Geronimo and his small band of people.[18]

So great was the "paranoia," that even after Geronimo surrendered, and in violation of the truce agreement, he and his followers were sent to prisons in Florida. This was a devastating situation for the Apache, not only because of the drastic climatic changes which were so physiologically damaging, but also because of the great psychological effect on the Indians. This can best be explained by quoting Geronimo himself:

> For each tribe of man Usen created He also made a home. In the land for any particular tribe He placed whatever would be best for the welfare of that tribe.
>
> When Usen created the Apaches He also gave them their homes in the West. He gave them such grain, fruits, and game

as they needed to eat — He gave them a pleasant climate and all they needed for clothing and shelter was at hand.

Thus it was in the beginning: The Apaches and their homes, each created for the other by Usen Himself. When they are taken from these homes they sicken and die.[19]

And thus many Apache died, not only the members of Geronimo's band but many others including some of the White Mountain and Chiricahua Apache scouts who captured Geronimo and were "rewarded" by imprisonment with him. They were kept in this prison environment for 28 years, until 1914, for the crime of defending their homes and land and their rights to freedom of movement. Finally they were released and allowed to go "home," but "home" no longer existed, so they ended up on the San Carlos Apache Indian Reservation in Arizona.

Geronimo, however, did not live to go home for he was killed in an accident in 1909 and buried at Fort Sill, Oklahoma. There are persistent rumors that his body was transported secretly back to his homeland by his loyal disciples, but there is no confirmation to this.

By the end of the 1870s, most of the Apache had been moved to the reservations on which they are still located. Anthropologists have grouped these people into six major divisions: the Western Apache, the Chiricahua Apache, the Mescalero Apache, the Jicarilla Apache, the Lipan Apache, and the Kiowa Apache. These divisions, which were so fiercely independent in the past, still maintain much of their autonomy, even though a degree of conglomeration has taken place on the reservation.

Today the Western Apache are located principally on the Fort Apache and San Carlos Reservations in Arizona, while the Jicarilla and the Mescalero have their own reservations in New Mexico. The Lipan and the Chiricahua are scattered on several reservations and do not maintain tribal identity with the federal government, but are noted according to the reservation on which they live. The Kiowa Apache are located in Oklahoma and identify generally with their adopted Plains relatives. A few Western Apache moved to the Camp Verde Reservation where they live with the Yavapai. For the most part, these reservations were areas of land in which the whites had little or no interest and on which it was thought the Apache would be out of the way of the settlers.

## FORT APACHE RESERVATION

Established on June 7, 1897 by dividing the San Carlos Reservation, Fort Apache Reservation was set aside for the White Mountain Apache people. This reservation was isolated pretty well from the rest of the world, accessible only by primitive trails, and restricted to travel on foot or horseback. Then, after much deliberation, a progressive tribal council agreed that if the tribe were ever to be economically viable, things must change. These Apache leaders were also aware of the possible erosion of their culture, so as plans were made to open the reservation, careful consideration was also given to the preservation of the Apache way of life. They adopted the Apache phrase "Hon-Dah," meaning "welcome" as their slogan and developed their homeland into what has been termed, "the largest privately-owned recreation area in the United States."

Utilizing the runoff from their snow-capped mountains, the tribe constructed numerous dams which now form twenty-six of the finest trout-fishing lakes in the world. Along the more than 420 miles of streams, they have built over 1000 camping sites with toilet and garbage facilities, and they maintain a network of access roads. For guests interested in staying a while, the tribe has motel units, apartments, and trailer parks as well as service stations and stores to provide for the needs of the visitors.

Sunrise Resort Park, on the eastern edge of the reservation, provides the best ski slopes in the state, a plush year-round hotel, a well-stocked fishing lake, miles of hiking and riding trails, and the finest weather for outdoor activities. Cultural attractions and tourist entertainment also take place throughout the year, and the White Mountain Apache have something for everyone each season of the year.

The Apache have not limited their economic progress to tourism though, but have diversified to provide a stable economic base for their tribal operations. Today their multimillion dollar tribally owned sawmill (Fort Apache Timber Company) is the area's largest employer. The annual output, if cut to two-by-four lumber and laid end to end, would encircle the globe with enough left over to reach from the reservation to the equator.

The leasing of hundreds of cabin home-sites called for the creation of a construction enterprise. This program was started at Hawley Lake, one of their best fishing lakes, where more than 500 sites were leased to people from all walks of life desiring a second home where they could escape the harried metropolitan pace.

The White Mountain Apache also manage and care for a herd of over 20,000 head of some of the finest beef cattle to be found anywhere. They graze on the lush grasses of the high meadows in the summer and utilize the well-developed winter pastures during the cold months. Supplemental hay and grains are raised on the irrigated and dry-farmed Apache land. This well-managed herd helps fill the treasury and assists in keeping this tribe independent of the paternalism of the federal government and free to exercise their own prerogatives.

The future of the White Mountain Apache appears to be most promising. A modern Apache is emerging and is creating a strong middle-class economy without sacrificing the cultural heritage. Apacheness is still very much alive at Fort Apache and is evident in every activity of the day. These people have learned to live in twentieth-century America without losing the qualities which have helped them survive through centuries of extreme pressures and genocidal endeavors. It is most remarkable that they can still say, "Hon-Dah," "Welcome, be my guest."

### SAN CARLOS RESERVATION

The San Carlos Indian Reservation was established on November 9, 1871 and the charter revised on December 14, 1872 as a dumping ground and concentration camp for a number of bands of Apache, along with groups of other Indians from Arizona. Disregarding the wants or needs, as well as the welfare, of the Indians, authorities chose to crowd these varied groups together simply for their own convenience. This naturally caused much friction between the different groups, some of which had been natural enemies for centuries, and the first few years of the reservation's history were quite hectic and far from peaceful. Removal of some of the groups to other reservations helped but in no way put an end to the unrest. With the fiercely independent Apache leaders in residence against their wills, it was not until Geronimo's surrender in 1886 that things permanently calmed down.

After the division which established the Fort Apache Reservation, San Carlos still had a vast expanse of land, 1,853,841 acres, much of which was of little use to the Indians. The southwestern portion was desert land, eroded by dry washes and orroyos, and the northern portion consisted of high mountains and canyons which, at that time, meant nothing to the people. The central and southeastern portions did give them a few basic places to start their program for survival. Although the San Carlos Apache have not experienced the economic development of the White Mountain Band, they have utilized the limited natural resources of the reservation to some extent.

In 1930, the federal government dedicated Coolidge Dam which confined the water from the Gila River and several smaller streams into San Carlos Lake. It is the largest and best-known water-sports area on the reservation, with its beautiful deep blue water a startling contrast to the starkness of the surrounding desert-canyon country. This lake, along with Point of Pines Lake and several ponds and streams, provides the tribe with some income from recreational activities. Some of the water is used for irrigation, especially for hay and pasture lands, for the San Carlos Apache are heavily involved in cattle raising.

Huge sections of the reservation were leased by non-Indian cattle companies until 1933. At that time the leases were canceled and the Indians began to develop their own cattle industry. Today there are five Apache associations of cattle raisers which specialize in producing some of the finest purebreed Hereford cattle to be found anywhere. This provides the tribe with its largest source of income.

Tourist attractions, other than fishing and hunting, also provide some income to the tribe. The San Carlos Apache still practice some ceremonials and dances — just as do their relatives to the north, the White Mountain Apache — some of which are open to the public. The most popular of these is the famous Sunrise, or "Puberty" ceremony, which in both Apache groups marks the coming of age of the girls of the tribe. The ritual is performed to entreat the spirits to provide the participants with long and happy lives. These ceremonials are generally held on weekends during the summer.

Each year, over the Veteran Day weekend in October, the San Carlos Apache hold their tribal rodeo and fair. This is an important occasion and many visitors come to the reservation at that time. The Indian "cowboys" of the tribe put on a good exhibition of riding and roping, and several ceremonial dances are held in conjunction with the other activities. These tourist-oriented presentations make a sizable contribution to the tribal treasury.

A few small business ventures by the tribe, as well as by some individual Apache, are beginning to be initiated to stimulate the economy on the reservation. The San Carlos Apache are definitely on the move and developing economic independence which follows the "self-determination" philosophy espoused by the Indian people and promoted by the federal government.

### JICARILLA RESERVATION

The Jicarilla Apache who occupy a reservation in northwestern New Mexico are a related group. They are one of the tribes which belong to the great Athapaskan linguistic stock, but with the Lipan, constitute a group which seems to be quite distinct from the other Apache.

There is little doubt that the Jicarilla traveled southward from northwestern Canada and Alaska as did the other Apachean people. They were probably a part of the Querecho met by Coronado during his trek across the Southwest in the 1540s. The first mention of them as a separate group was made by Juan de Ulabarri about 1706. They received their name from their artwork, for Jicarilla is a Spanish word meaning "little baskets."

In 1733 a Spanish mission was built for them near Taos, New Mexico but the Jicarilla were not very interested in the Catholic religious training, so it did not last very long. In general, the Spanish found the Jicarilla quite hostile and had little success in their association.

The United States government also met with failure in dealing with these people, for they were fiercely intent on living in their homeland and wanted no part of new locations proposed by the Indian Bureau. They were the last American Indian tribe to be permanently settled on a reservation, when in 1887 they were placed, starving and indigent, on the lands they now occupy.

Forced to stay in this alien area, the Jicarilla felt they would all perish, and they did indeed begin to die. They had been a vibrant, healthy people when they were confined, but by 1914, ninety percent of the tribe was afflicted with tuberculosis and the people were dying so fast that officials predicted the tribe would be extinct by 1932. Not only were they physically ill, but they had lost interest in everything about them, and even lost the will to live. It was not until sheep were introduced to the reservation that the Jicarilla showed any promise of survival. Economic progress began and physical health started to improve.

A boarding school was established at Dulce, the tribal head-quarters in the northeastern corner of the reservation, and education was introduced. The facilities were used interchangeably as a school and tuberculosis sanitarium until 1940 when the sanitarium was finally closed, and the buildings used exclusively for educational purposes.

Besides advancing educationally and improving in health, the Jicarilla, like their other Apache relatives, began economic development with the concept of self-dependency. They exploited the natural resources of the reservation to the fullest and initiated tourist attractions which would stabilize the economic situation. Eight lakes now dot the scenic area, five of which are well-stocked with rainbow trout. These are open to the public as is a section of the Navajo River which traverses Jicarilla land. Wild game abounds and these attractions draw visitors from all over the West.

The tribe has modernized its towns with water and sewage lines, allocation of urban home sites, zoning, and other community developments. Income from the excellent stands of timber are now supplemented by royalties from oil and gas production. Commercial endeavors are springing up all over the reservation in the form of supermarkets, banks, cafes, motels, and other enterprises.

With this activity, and much more planned for the future, the Jicarilla Apache are well on the way toward economic self-sufficiency and a perpetuation of the typical Apache independence.

## MESCALERO RESERVATION

The Mescalero Apache live on a reservation of about 460,000 acres of beautiful mountain land in the southeastern part of New Mexico. Their history parallels that of their relatives, as related earlier, with hostilities and depredations perpetrated by the invading Europeans, starting with the Spaniards in the sixteenth century.

The first recorded fighting that occurred between the Spanish and the Mescalero was in 1590 when Gaspar Castano de Sosa killed a few Apache and enslaved several others. This established the policy which was followed throughout the Spanish period in the Southwest. Apache were fair game for murder and to provide slaves to perform the manual labor for the building of the Spanish colonial empire. The Mescalero, along with the other bands, were included in this pattern of physical exploitation.

The genocidal operation of the Spaniards was not carried on easily, however, or without strong opposition from and retaliation by the Apache. Attempts by the clergy to convert the

Mescalero to Catholicism were little more successful than those of the military. The fierce independence of the people and their faith in their way of life made it impossible to reduce them to vassals of the Church or any other entity of the Spanish government. After the acquisition of the Southwest from Mexico by the United States in 1848, things did not change appreciably. The greatest alteration was restricted to the presence of a new oppressor. Tactics in dealing with the Apache were carried on as if no change had occurred and, if anything changed at all, it was an accelerated genocidal thrust by the Americans.

During the Civil War, about 400 Mescalero Apache were taken prisoner by the United States Army and confined to a forty-square-mile tract of land on the Pecos River known as Bosque Redondo. Brigadier James H. Carleton was appointed military commander of New Mexico and he set out to "civilize" these prisoners. He directed agricultural activities by developing irrigation systems and utilized modern techniques in an attempt to make the Apache become farmers. This might have met with some success if Carleton had used intelligent planning, honest administration, and a degree of common sense. Of course, none of these attributes was utilized by the captors. Unilateral decision making, with little thought given to the culture or traditions of the prisoners, was the policy used by Carleton.

Restricting the people to the reservation, not even allowing mescal-gathering parties, and forcing the Indians to subsist on the meager products of mismanaged farms was definitely courting disaster. Then, as if the situation were not bad enough, Carleton moved over 8000 Navajo, traditional enemies of the Mescalero, to Bosque Redondo to share the area with the Apache. This was too much for the Mescalero who had been attempting to maintain peaceful relations with the army in spite of overwhelming negative forces.

Even if the Navajo and Mescalero had been on amicable terms, the land could not support the large force of captives. Seeing the futility of the situation, the Mescalero held secret councils and, on the night of November 3, 1865, they simply vanished.

To this day, no white person knows where they spent the following years. Finally, on May 29, 1873, an executive order set aside the present reservation in their traditional mountain homeland in New Mexico. This was not the end of their troubles, but they were able to hold on.

In recent years, through aggressive and far-sighted leadership, they have developed their reservation economically while at the same time strenuously maintaining their cultural integrity which has enabled them to survive the pressures of the past 400 years.

The Mescalero Apache began their economic initiative in 1956 when Apache Summit was opened to the public. This tourist complex included a service station, restaurant, curio shop, and motel with picturesque log cabins nestled in the pines. Located at the top of the 8000-foot pass between Mescalero and the summer resort town of Ruidoso, the endeavor had all the qualities to ensure success, except one — the timing was premature. The tribespeople were not quite ready for such an ambitious venture as their first step toward entry into the modern business world. After about ten years of struggling, the tribe leased the enterprise to a private contractor who experienced no success, and the entire operation was closed soon afterward.[20]

This experience was viewed only as a temporary setback by the tribe and, with typical Apache resolution, they explored other avenues to financial stability. Under the direction of Wendell Chino, the long-time, aggressive and progressive President of the Mescalero Tribe, they attempted other commercial endeavors. Some were successful and some were not, but the Mescalero people, displaying typical Apache determination, continued their efforts.

These have paid off, for the Mescalero Apache Tribe is now financially successful and is establishing itself as a viable institution in today's business world. The acquisition of Ski Enterprises where hundreds of skiers congregate on the slopes of Sierra Blanca, the tourist complex of the Inn of the Mountain Gods, and other attractions, places the reservation high on the list of tourist centers. The development of natural resources, timber industries, and cattle raising also provides income for the tribal treasury as well as for the individual Mescalero.

All four of the Apache reservations, Fort Apache, San Carlos, Jicarilla, and Mescalero are demonstrating the resilience and adaptability of the "People called Apache." Coming from a point of near extermination to the functional units of today, these people have illustrated to the world their remarkable capabilities. As they have been allowed some freedom of choice in this decade of Indian self-determination, they have developed their resources and firmly established themselves as viable units of government which will continue regardless of the vacillation of political units within the structure of the United States.

# 7
# Hopi

The Hopi, whose name is derived from their own Uto-Aztecan word for themselves, Hopituh, which means "the peaceful ones," trace their ancestry back to the Anasazi culture and their history as a people back many thousands of years. Oral tradition tells of an emergence from the underworld, the destruction of three prior worlds, the Great Flood, and many other happenings which make them an ancient people. Some of these stories stand under close scrutiny by anthropologists and "New World" historians, and some, as with traditions of most peoples, must be accepted with faith as the only supportive evidence. These stories, which have existed for untold generations, tell the Hopi that their ancestors wandered for centuries looking for a place where the vibrations were good and their crops would grow. They came from the north country and tried many places before finding their present homeland. It is there on the mesas of northern Arizona that the Hopi claim is the vibrational center for the entire planet.

Their first contact with Europeans was in 1540 when two of the Coronado expedition members, Pedro de Tobar and Juan de Padilla, visited them. They found the Hopi living a life-style much like that of their Anasazi ancestors. They had multi-storied apartment-style houses perched on the edge of high mesas, and they were tilling their fields of corn, squash, and beans in the areas below the cliffs.

The Spaniards brought many new items which the Hopi quickly adopted. Metal tools, weapons, and furniture were utilized in a very short time, and agricultural innovations supplemented the Hopi diet as they grew tomatoes, onions, and peaches. Cattle and sheep provided new sources of protein, the hides were used to make clothing, and the wool from the sheep furnished material for weaving. These bearded strangers also introduced horses and burros which greatly extended Hopi travel and increased their trade area.

The Hopi, although they sometimes resented the Spanish intrusion, remained at peace and even allowed Catholic missionaries to establish churches in several communities. These missions were allowed to remain for about 50 years, even though they caused friction among the Hopi, for they were viewed as a threat to the traditional way of life by many of the people.

In 1680 the entire Pueblo population in New Mexico revolted and drove the Spaniards out of the area. The Hopi joined the revolt and destroyed all the Catholic churches and other buildings on the mesas. In 1699 the Spanish regained control of Pueblo-land and reestablished a mission at the village of Awatovi with no opposition from the villagers. The traditional Hopi, however, were so enraged that they attacked the village, killed most of the men, relocated the women and children, and allowed the village to slowly collapse into ruin. Only a few of its clans and ceremonies survive in other villages.

Fearing Spanish retaliation, the lower villages were moved to the top of the mesas where all sites were reinforced and made more defensible. Since the Hopi were such peaceful people and did not want to engage in conflict, they hired a group of the more aggressive Tewa to defend their homes. The descendants of these Tewa mercenaries still live in the village of Hano on the top of First Mesa.

Over the first 300 or so years of contact with the whites, the Hopi people suffered terrible catastrophes which nearly destroyed them.  Besides the ever-present threat of raids from the Navajo, Ute, and Apache, the Hopi were decimated by diseases brought by the Europeans.  Since these were new maladies, the Hopi people had no natural resistance to them and the results were disastrous.

In 1643, the Hopi numbered around 14,000 people and an outbreak of smallpox brought by the Spanish killed over 11,000 of them.  The population was rebuilt, but in 1780–81, another outbreak struck and left only about 900 people alive.  In 1853–54 the deadly disease again ravaged Hopiland killing about 6,000 of the 8,000 people.

At the conclusion of the Mexican War in 1848, the United States acquired the Hopi homeland as a part of the settlement outlined in the Treaty of Guadalupe Hidalgo.  Soon after this travesty, the United States government began all-out efforts, which continue to this day, to acculturate and "civilize" the Hopi.  The leaders of the tribe resisted such things as their children being forced to attend white schools and other activities they thought were designed to destroy Hopi culture.  To bring these dissident leaders in line and in order to make examples of them, many were imprisoned for their resistance.

Eventually some of the Hopi began to succumb to the demands of white society.  They sent their children to school, changed their mode of dress, adopted Christianity and, in general, abandoned the things which gave them the strength to hold off the Spanish and Mexican attempts for 300 years.  This change in attitude brought on a schism in the Hopi Nation which exists to this day.  The division between the "traditionals" and the "progressives" permeates Hopi society and prevents united action by the tribe on nearly all issues.  The ancient tactic of "divide and conquer" is still working with the Hopi as it is with many other tribes.

After the introduction of the Indian Reorganization Act of 1934,[21] the Hopi were further fragmented by the United States government.   They were forced to organize a tribal council, supposedly representative of the tribe as a whole. Some of the villages refused to participate in this nontraditional form of government, claiming it would be compromising their ancient religion and culture.   As pressures continue to be exerted from various agencies, governmental, religious, and societal, more Hopi succumb.   The tribal council is assuming more control as time passes, but it still faces considerable resistance from the conservative faction of the tribe.

Today the Hopi Reservation exemplifies a dual state of existence.   While many of the old customs prevail and even thrive, some are undergoing changes and others have disappeared completely.   Old villages still bustle with everyday activity carried out in the same manner as it has been for generations. Visitors are excluded because of the negative experience the Hopi have had with tourists. Ceremonials are conducted in an extremely sacred manner and, except for a few modern implements, time stands still. The inhabitants hold to their life-styles which have withstood the trials of time, and proudly maintain their centuries-old customs.

Hopi farmers today plant their fields of corn, squash, beans, and melons with the use of a planting stick, a method that was used by their ancestors at least as long ago as 300 B.C. While many of the villages retain the appearance of ancient pueblos with their plazas, kivas, and hand-hewn stone buildings, close by some of these are modern villages whose appearance and activities are little different from those of hundreds of small non-Indian villages throughout the Southwest.

Most Hopi live in twelve villages on the reservation which are located on the top or at the foot of three mesas, First Mesa, Second Mesa, and Third Mesa. These three flat-topped protuberances extend out from the huge, sacred Black Mesa like gigantic thick fingers. Most of the homes on the top are built of stone, logs, and mud and are very old, while those at the lower elevation are much newer and made of more modern materials.

At the eastern end of the Hopi Reservation is the town of Keams Canyon.  This is not a Hopi village although it does house the Hopi Indian Agency and is headquarters for much of the federal bureaucracy which controls the activities on the reservation. All but a few of the buildings are owned by the federal government.

About fifteen miles west of Keams Canyon is First Mesa with the town of Polacca at the foot of the mesa and the villages of Hano, Walpi, and Sichomovi located on the top. Walpi is a ceremonial village and looks the same as it has for centuries. The town, like the ceremonies it houses, has remained unchanged, impervious to the turmoil of changing times. The Tewa village of Hano and the pueblo Sichomovi are better known for their production of arts and crafts.

Second Mesa lies about ten miles west of First Mesa, on the top of which are the villages of Shungopovi, Shipaulovi, and Mishongonovi. Nestling at the foot of the cliffs of Second Mesa is the tiny village of Toreva, inhabited primarily by Christianized Hopi and not considered a Hopi settlement by the traditional people.

On Third Mesa, a few miles further west, are the towns of Bacavi, Hotevilla, and Old Oraibi, the oldest continuously inhabited community in the United States. At the foot of Third Mesa is New Oraibi, headquarters for the Hopi tribal government.

The westernmost village on the reservation is Moenkopi, about forty-five miles from Hotevilla, near the Navajo settlement of Tuba City. Moenkopi is a typical Hopi village, nestling in a small canyon with its houses made of stone and adobe. There are small farms and orchards scattered about in the flat areas among the sand dunes where the Hopi farmers pursue their vocation in the same way their forefathers have done for centuries.

The Hopi are a quiet and private people but genuinely friendly toward those who display courtesy and respect for their traditions. Because of the "ugly American" approach and arrogant and discourteous actions by large numbers of tourists, some of the villages have been ruled off-limits to non-Hopi. A number of ceremonies and dances are also restricted to Indians because of the behavior of non-Indian visitors when they were allowed

to attend.  The Hopi are still rather conservative in their accep-
tance of tourism as a business, and visitors are requested to
abide by Hopi rules and to respect Hopi feelings.

The most obvious and striking evidence of the preservation
of Hopi culture lies in their religious ceremonies.  Among the
most important and surely the most famous of the Hopi ceremonials is the Snake Dance.  It is also perhaps the most misunderstood by the general public.  The dance is actually a
prayer for rain to ensure a corn crop on which Hopi survival,
so precariously balanced, depends.  It is held in August of
alternating years in participating villages and depicts a unique
relationship between the Hopi and the snakes who act as
messengers to the deities.  This sacred ceremony was once
open to visitors, but because of the abuses of hospitality and
sacrilegious behavior during the dances, it is now closed to
tourists.

Some ceremonies are still open and are usually presented on
weekends in the plaza.  Those which are not public are held in
the kivas, underground ceremonial houses, which only those
who have been through the initiation ritual may attend.

Each clan of the tribe has its own dances and rituals and
these generally last for several days.  They are held for the
benefit of all and are supplications for rain and to maintain
the tribe's harmony with the natural forces around it.  It is
quite disconcerting that so many visitors fail to comprehend
or appreciate the sacredness of these occasions, and increasing
numbers of the ceremonies are being restricted.  The very conservative elements among the people strongly resent the lack of
respect displayed by outsiders.

Some of the dances are more social than sacred and tourists
are welcome to attend and even participate on a limited basis.
The kachina ceremonies are in this category and are enjoyed by
many non-Indians, for they are the most beautiful and colorful
of all Hopi rituals.  The ornately decorated dancers represent
supernatural spirits, some of which are considered as gods and
others as intermediaries between man and greater spirits.  The
kachinas may also be represented by dolls carved from the root

of the cottonwood tree.  They are presented to children during kachina ceremonies as tokens of friendship between the kachinas and the Hopi.  Many kachina dolls are made for sale to tourists by Hopi artisans and have become valuable collectors' items throughout North America.

Since about 1970, the Hopi have begun to capitalize on tourism, and today, directly or indirectly, it provides a major portion of the income for the tribe and for many individual Hopi people.  Hopi basketry has become widely recognized for its beauty, and many coiled and plaited baskets are made and sold.  Since they are some of the best made of any Indian baskets, Hopi basketmakers keep busy year-round turning out their ornate products.

Using the ancient method of coiling clay into desired shapes, then polishing it to a lustrous finish, Hopi potters create a variety of beautiful bowls and pots.  Decorations are in the form of ancient symbols found on old pottery and have caught the eye of visitors and collectors from all over the world.  Local plants and minerals provide the coloring used in painting the designs and the ceramics are then fired using sheep manure as fuel.

Jewelry-making has been a tradition in Hopi culture for centuries, but not until the late nineteenth century did they begin to use silver in their work.  These artisans have gained fame for their beautiful overlay work with silver and gemstones.  Current innovations in Hopi jewelry include work in gold rather than silver and setting diamonds and other precious stones.

Hopi painting has become popular in recent times and a number of Hopi artists have gained fame.  The depiction of kachinas, either alone or in groups, is the most popular motif, but paintings showing other features of Hopi life have become increasingly prominent in recent years.

For centuries, Hopi have been famous for their textile weaving, not only in the form of fabrics for everyday wear, but also for ornately woven ceremonial pieces.  Today it is a rapidly fading craft and few are engaged in it.  The small amount of weaving that is done is primarily for ceremonial use, but occasionally one of the weavers produces a highly prized article for sale.

Income for the Hopi tribe, as stated earlier, depends greatly on tourism. There are a number of small private businesses to be found on the reservation, but these do not play a major part in the overall Hopi economy. Employment by the tribe and the federal government provides income to many members and helps a fairly stable economy for the Hopi. The tribe recently built a Cultural Center complex on Second Mesa with a hotel, restaurant, campground, and arts and crafts shops. This installation has stimulated tourism by providing modern conveniences and, as a result, has brought added emphasis to the popularizing of Hopi arts and crafts.

While the Hopi are gaining in their economic struggle, all is not peaceful with these people. As alluded to earlier, there is political unrest within the tribe because of the division between the progressives and the traditionalists. Another disturbing factor is the problem of the "joint use" portion of the Hopi Reservation. The Hopi Reservation actually comprises 1,561,213 acres but only 631,194 acres is available for the sole use of the Hopi. The balance is set aside to be used jointly by them and the Navajo. This arrangement was made in 1882 by President Chester A. Arthur by presidential decree in an effort to settle "the Indian problem."

Things did not go as President Arthur had envisioned and the Navajo moved in and occupied most of the area. Since the early 1960s battles have been waged in courts, bills have been introduced in Congress, and Hopi and Navajo leaders have talked about military confrontations and "bluecoats."[22] With all this, the situation remains as an ominous cloud on the peaceful scene in Hopiland.

Another situation faces the Hopi people which has many grave consequences and poses the most serious threat, philosophically and spiritually, if not politically. At the northern end of Black Mesa a huge power plant has been constructed with a strip-mining operation to supply it with coal. Although the industry is located on Navajo land, the Hopi have an important relationship to the project. They consider themselves to be stewards of their ancient homeland, of which Black Mesa

Hopi Culture Center, Oraibi, Arizona

is the center.  The Great Spirit has charged them with the responsibility of preserving this land, which they consider to be the spiritual center of the universe.  Hopi prophecy says that if the sacred lands are ruined, the world will end.  The desecration of the Black Mesa land through strip-mining, and the building of roads, transmission lines, and railroads, violates the central tenets of Hopi culture and tradition.

Although Hopi and Navajo are usually not in accord, the traditional members of both tribes concur completely on this issue.  The beauty and harmony of their natural surroundings is a basic tenet of Navajo belief, and Black Mesa plays a special role in the Navajo drama of creation.  Traditional Navajo believe that the spirits and gods of their sacred mountains created man from his natural surroundings.[23]  The traditional leaders from both tribes have vigorously opposed the power project and have enlisted the aid of many people and organizations, Indian and non-Indian, in an effort to preserve their sacred ground, but to no avail.  The smoke still blots out the sun, the ash still pollutes thousands of acres of land, and the sacred earth is still being raped by the machines of industrialized America.

The spiritual and philosophical difficulties initiated by this strip-mining and power-plant operation are not the only problem for the Hopi and other tribes.  The ecological disruption could have disastrous ramifications.

Peabody Coal Company of St. Louis, Missouri, a wholly owned subsidiary of Kennecott Copper Company, is the sole supplier of coal to the Navajo Generating Station built at Page, Arizona, and at least a partial provider to other power plants in the Southwest.  Peabody is using open-cut (strip-mining) techniques to extract huge quantities of the mineral which is transported by train to the plants.  Various techniques have been utilized to help make this operation more economically feasible.  One of these is the attempt to negotiate contracts for multiple plants which will cut the overall cost.  Peabody has been quite successful in this venture.

Another technique which has also proven economically sound is the use of the largest earth-moving shovel in the country.  The gigantic machine has a bucket large enough to remove 130 cubic yards of material with each "bite." This allows enormous amounts of earth to be removed quite rapidly and at a much lower cost than "shaft-mining."

With this shovel, it may be possible to mine up to 300 feet deep in the Mesa Verde sandstone which covers the area and contains veins of coal as thick as 65 feet. The machine also has the capability of cutting even deeper into and through the 150 to 300-foot thick Mancos shale underlying the sandstone. This shale also contains smaller seams of coal, which are still profitable for mining. Below the shale is Dakota sandstone, varying from less than 20 feet to as much as 300 feet in thickness. Here the seams of coal, interspersed with thin shale and sandstone, are as much as 65 feet thick. In some areas of Black Mesa erosion has brought these valuable strata close enough to the earth's surface to be mined with the huge shovel.

The mining and associated power-plant operations consume unbelievable amounts of water, and much of this necessarily comes from the underground reservoirs at Black Mesa which were filled eons ago and recharge only at a very slow rate from groundwater seepage. The pumping for industrial use and accelerated leaking through shafts drilled in the slowly permeable shale, added to the damage done by the giant machines, leads to a deaquafication of all the water-storage basins.

Since the underground water is available on Hopi farmlands by springs and seeps, and because this water runs north to south and the reservoirs lie north of the Hopi, disturbances which affect the reservoir level have a very bad effect on Hopi agriculture.

Toxic effects from chemicals produced and released in the air by burning coal is well known. Sulphur dioxide, carbon monoxide, and other gasses are emitted in enormous quantities by the power plants, and have produced health hazards for the Indians.

Because the smoke stacks at the Page plant are 700 to 800 feet high, the solid-waste particles do not quickly fall to earth but remain in the air for some time. Such an occluded atmosphere

Hopi cornfield — agriculture methods have not changed for centuries

can dangerously affect the growing season on Black Mesa and in Hopi country. Since this growing season is only about 100 days in length and frost-free nights number about 130, agriculture for the Hopi is on a very tight schedule. If late frosts in the spring and early frosts in the fall keep occurring because of increased numbers of solid particles in the atmosphere, agriculture in the Black Mesa-Hopi area will cease.

This situation is much more serious and threatening to traditional Hopi than all other threats combined, for their very existence is at stake. Many Hopi prophesies have come to pass, as have many from other religions, so it remains to be seen what happens. In the meantime, the Hopi Nation is making progress toward modernization of some facets of their activities, while tenaciously holding on to much of their ancient spirituality and practices. Truly, the present-day Hopi is inhabiting two worlds.

# 8
# Zuni, Acoma, and Laguna

## ZUNI

As noted in Chapter 1, the Zuni Indians of New Mexico are the only known descendants of the Mogollon culture. The ancestry of the Zuni is undoubtedly mixed with other groups because of extremely unstable conditions in the Southwest prior to the arrival of the Europeans. The great drought period of 1276–99 necessitated a relocation of many people to areas with an adequate water supply, and one of these was the Zuni territory. Other groups moved to escape the harassment of nomadic tribes and surely some of these moved in with the Zuni. The cruelty of European invaders forced population patterns to change drastically and undoubtedly, this also affected the Zuni.

Zuni was the first of the southwestern pueblos to be sighted by Europeans. Gold-hungry Spaniards, excited by stories of the fabulously wealthy "Seven Cities of Cibola" sent an exploration party from Mexico to the north in 1539. This group was under the leadership of Father Marcos de Niza, a Franciscan priest, and was guided by a huge Barbary black man called Esteban. Reaching the Zuni village of Hawikuh, Esteban, dressed in gaudy attire with slaves preceding him to demand tribute, was killed for his arrogance and indiscretions. Father Marcox, hearing of Esteban's fate left for Mexico where he spread extravagant stories of the great riches he had discovered. The famous Coronado expedition followed Marcos's trail and encountered the Zuni people in 1540.

On the first meeting of these two races, fighting broke out and a hatred developed between them which lasts to this day. As the Spaniards entered Hawikuh, the reported golden city, they found only mud and stone huts, unfriendly natives, and no gold. The Zuni had removed their women and children to the summit of Corn Mountain, a 1000-foot-high nearly inaccessible butte a few miles east of the village and a fortress to which the men soon retreated. The avaricious Spaniards, bitterly disappointed at not finding gold, ravaged the Rio Grande pueblos and even moved out into the Plains. There, too, they found none of the riches they sought, and, after two years of fruitless searching, withdrew to Mexico, leaving bitter memories for the Indian People.

Other Spanish expeditions visited the Zuni, using their traditional cruel and heartless methods, until 1680 when the Zuni joined the other pueblos in revolt. The Spanish were either killed or driven out of the territory and the Zuni again moved to Corn Mountain where they stayed until de Vargas conquered the Pueblos and reinstated Spanish control in 1693.

These actions by the Spaniards caused a persistent resistance by the Zuni toward Christianity, and they still have a strong distrust and suspicion of Mexicans, the descendants of the hated Spanish. Even to this day, Mexicans are barred from Zuni ceremonials and Christianity has never become a major element in the lives of the Zuni people.

As a consequence of the Mexican War, the United States acquired jurisdiction over the Zuni in 1848. At first, as with other Indian tribes, the Americans were welcomed by the Zuni people and an era of friendly relations existed. Over the years, however, the Indians gradually became disenchanted with the exploitation and duplicity of the government and the Anglo pioneers, missionaries, and others with whom they were compelled to deal. There is still a strong distrust by the tribesmen toward whites and the reaction is one of cautious and guarded interaction by the Zuni. Realizing that the only possibility for economic survival and, that to a great extent because the Bureau of Indian Affairs has extreme power over the Indian tribes in America, the Zuni carry out their dealings with veiled secrecy and reserve. Influence from Christian missionary pressure has never had a great effect on the Zuni people and, even with the efforts of the Spanish Catholics and the American Protestants, the Zuni have maintained much of their ancient traditional way of life and their religious integrity. Their culture persists as it has for centuries, with only the modifications necessary to function and survive in today's world.

The Zuni are a very independent and unique people. As stated earlier, they are the only known descendants of the Mogollon culture. They have withstood the pressures to acculturate and assimilate, and even their language, which is very much alive today, is singular in the world. They, along with the Yuchi of the Southeast, have a unique language which does not fit into any known linguistic family. For many years linguists and anthropologists have diligently researched in an attempt to solve this puzzle, but to no avail. In spite of their efforts only feeble postulates have been advanced, and no acceptable answer to the mystery has been found. The Zuni are just different.

Their religious rituals, while they share many aspects of other pueblo religions, are also unique in themselves. The Zuni, who are sometimes called the most thoroughly religious people on earth, center much of their thought and endeavor around an elaborate series of rites designed to win divine blessings. Every phase of Zuni life is permeated with the ceremonial of the religion and is oriented around religious observances.

In Zuni religion there is one basic cult, the Cult of the Ancestors, in which every Zuni participates. From that foundation six other more esoteric cults have developed. These include the Cult of the Sun, the Cult of the Priests of the Kachinas, the Cult of the War Gods, the Cult of the Rainmakers (Uwanami), the Cult of the Kachinas, and the Cult of the Beast Gods with its twelve medicine societies.   Each of the six cults has its priest-hoods, its fetishes, its places of worship, its secret rituals, and its calendar of time in the worship of particular supernatural beings.  The basic Cult of the Ancestors is nonesoteric and does not include a priesthood or priviledged membership, but does play a part in every ceremony and in the worship of all other cults.  Zuni oral tradition also plays an important part in every-day activity and provides symbols which have kept the people together for so long.[24]

The most popular cult at Zuni, and the one most people recognize, is the Kachina cult.[25]  All male members of the tribe, and a few females, are initiated into the Kachina society and are required to participate in its ceremonies.  The cult is highly organized into six divisions each with its priests and has a strong effect on the life of every Zuni.

The first kachinas are believed to be children who were lost long ago while fording a stream and were transformed into beautiful and happy beings who now live under the waters of Whispering Waters, the Sacred Lake.  Some are also considered to be spirits of the dead, for deceased members of the Kachina Cult go to live with them in their spirit world.  There all the kachinas spend their time singing and dancing and return to visit Zuni once each year during the fall.  While there, they are represented by the masked members of the Kachina cult who, when they put on the appropriate mask, are believed to be transformed into the particular kachina for the duration of the ceremony.  If the cult member dishonors the mask in any way, it is believed that it will stick to his face or choke him.  These masks, which are worn by the impersonators, are the vehicles which make the transformation possible and they have tre-mendous power.

The Zuni believe that all animals and natural forces such as the winds, the clouds, the rain, day and night, and even man-made objects are alive and have souls.  If man, who is the center of the universe, is to receive the blessings of the deities, the entire creation must be kept in harmonious balance by prayers, offerings, daily living practices, and appropriate ceremonies performed in prescribed ritual codes. Ritual techniques are, in essence, the Zuni's request for supernatural favor.

Economic development for the Zuni people has followed an erratic pattern and yet has been on an upward spiral since the late 1800s. The people have always been agricultural and have placed heavy emphasis on crops as the foundation for their sustenance. After the Spanish era, they supplemented their crop farming by raising livestock with an emphasis on sheep. Construction of dams by the federal government for irrigation of cropland had little effect on the Zuni for many of the farmers still grew their crops in the same dry-farming method used for centuries, and others were primarily interested in raising sheep and did not use the irrigation water.

During the Depression, they did show a little more interest in agricultural innovations and, for a while, crop production rose. Then World War II and the call for fighting men removed a large number of Zuni from the land and crop farming again declined. After the war, Zuni men were far more interested in raising sheep and making jewelry than in producing corn. The wages for these occupations far exceeded those of the "dirt farmer."

Silver crafting and jewelry making were learned from the Navajo in the 1800s. It was not too long before these apt pupils had developed their own method of inlaying shell and stone, and they surpassed their teachers in the production of a finer, more ornate quality of silversmithing. Although income from this craft has declined in recent years, Zuni smiths are using innovative approaches and sales are increasing. This work remains one of the main sources of tribal income.

Other craftwork has declined over the years, and today does not have a great effect on tribal economy. Zuni potters historically have produced extremely fine ceramics, but now Zuni pottery is nearly nonexistent. A few artisans still climb to the top of Corn Mountain to dig clay and proceed through the tedious operations involved in making the distinctive Zuni products, but not to the extent their ancestors did.

The men of the tribe were formerly excellent basketmakers, but this too has disappeared as a craft in the tribe. In past times, they made a variety of coarse utility baskets of willow and dogwood, including wicker carrying baskets and shallow winnowing trays. Plaited baskets were woven with yucca leaves and attached to a heavy wooden rim to provide the strength to contain the grain during the cleaning process. The Zuni of today purchase baskets from the Hopi and the Apache.

The men were also expert weavers in both wool and cotton, making women's dresses, kilts, sashes, belts, and a variety of ceremonial garments of elaborate design. This is now an abandoned art and the Zuni depend upon outside sources for these items. They even trade with the Hopi to obtain ceremonial garments to use in their spiritual observances.

With the income from tribal ventures in agriculture and sheep raising, and the substantial income derived from tourism and jewelry making, the Zuni are a prosperous people. The clean modern houses of the villages with the beehive ovens used for centuries to bake the pueblo bread reflect this prosperity and well-being. The Zuni people have found the narrow pathway between the Indian and the white worlds and have been able to extract the best from both. They have developed a synthesized culture that draws the materialistic conveniences from one to provide physical comforts, while retaining the aesthetic qualities of the other to ensure psychological and spiritual stability in their lives.

## ACOMA

Unlike their Zuni neighbors, the people of Acoma, the Sky City, have a pretty well-established cultural background, speak a language related to that of other tribes in the area, and seem to be an integral part of the evolution of groups in the Southwest. Evidently the Acoma descended from portions of the Anasazi culture, and during the period of severe drought in the thirteenth century, 1276–99, their population was mixed because of the migration of other Anasazi from northern cities. The Acoma do not question this, and claim they have always hospitably received wandering tribes and shared their valley which once had plenty of water and was excellent for farming. As with Indian tribes all over America, there are many theories as to the origin of the Acoma and how long they have occupied "the pueblo in the sky."[26] But it is agreed by all that Acoma has been an inhabited city for a very long time.

The first confirmed visit by a European was in August 1540 when Captain Hernando de Alvarado and Fray Juan Padilla recorded their encounter with the people of Acoma. Alvarado described the pueblo as one of the "strongest ever seen, because the city was built on a high rock." It was described by another Spaniard as "the greatest stronghold ever seen in the world." Although they did occupy an almost impregnable fortress, the Acaoma welcomed the Spaniards. This, as they would soon realize, was a mistake. The friendly attitude of the natives was experienced and recorded by numerous Spanish visitors until the fateful day of December 4, 1598.

On this day, a party of about thirty Spaniards, under the command of Captain Juan de Zaldivar, arrived at Acoma. They, too, were welcomed by the natives, but when they demanded tribute in excess of what the Acoma considered appropriate, they were attacked and Zaldivar and twelve others were killed.

An avenging company of seventy men was organized by Juan's brother, Vicente de Zaldivar, and arrived at Acoma on January 21, 1599. A three-day battle was waged, and after sustaining heavy losses, the Indian fortress fell. The fighting was fierce and losses were heavy on both sides, but the cruelest ordeal came after the battle was over and the Spaniards began their vindictive retaliation.

Seventy or eighty men were taken prisoner along with about 500 women and children. Many were imprisoned in the kivas, from which they were taken one at a time, murdered, and thrown over the cliff. Those who did not suffer this fate were herded to Santo Domingo Pueblo where don Juan de Oñate, the Spanish governor, presided over their trial. His verdict and punishment of the Indians was one of the harshest ever recorded. It was as follows:

The males over twenty-five years of age were sentenced to have one foot cut off and to serve twenty years slavery.

The males between twelve and twenty-five were to spend twenty years slavery.

The women over twelve years of age were sentenced to twenty years slavery.

Two Hopi Indians who participated in the battle had the right hand cut off and were set free so they could tell of the punishment in their own land.

All of the children under twelve years of age were held free of guilt, so in order to "protect" them, Oñate turned the girls over to Fray Alonzo Martinez and the boys to Vicente de Zalvidar, the conqueror of Acoma, so both boys and girls could "attain the knowledge of God and the salvation of their souls."

The old men and women, disabled in the "war" were turned over to the Querechas "that they may support them and ensure they would not leave the pueblo."

The sentences pronounced by Oñate were representative of the treatment by the Spanish of all the New World's native people. To salve its conscience, the Spanish crown did try and convict Oñate and Zaldivar for some of their crimes. But the sentences and fines of the two Spanish conquistadores were minimal tokens which allowed Spain to claim technically, that it was following a mandate of benevolence dictated by the Pope.

Acoma, although it played no important part in the 1680 revolt of the pueblos because of its isolation, did lend moral support to the Pueblo Indians of Rio Grande. When the revolt was over and Spain again ruled the Southwest, Acoma received a land grant from the government which established definite pueblo boundaries.

Over the next 150 years, the lives of the Acoma were manipulated by the Spanish, and then by the Mexican governments in political rather than military situations. The Apache had a telling effect on the residents of "Sky City" with their raids for horses and other stock, but the real threat to the Indians came in 1848. That year the Americans became the legal "protectors" of the Acoma. The Indians were exposed to bureaucratic machinations, harassment by settlers and pioneers, gold seekers, and ranchers, and constant pressures from the outside world which would have been even heavier if it were not for the geographic isolation of Acoma.

Throughout the early years of the twentieth century, Acoma was involved in economic battling and commercial maneuvering in the marketing of agricultural products. Being astute in bargaining and diversified in the products they raised, the Acoma Pueblo farmers became a power in agricultural and livestock production in the Southwest. Today, the Acoma are still using their land for agricultural purposes but the acute water shortage has forced a curtailment of land utilization. It has become increasingly clear that Acoma cannot develop the land and support a growing population without more water. The tribal officials are diligently pursuing a solution to this problem.

The Acoma religion is a strange mixture of centuries-old tribal ceremonies and imported Catholicism. The people have held their traditional rituals in the plaza since ancient times. Each year they hold harvest and feast-day dances.

Most of these ceremonies are deeply sacred and are closed to the public. They have not received the attention and publicity of the Zuni and Hopi dances which are open, or have been open at one time, to the public. They are, however, as spiritually oriented and as influential in Acoma life as are the ceremonies of other tribes.

On September 2, the Acoma depart from their tribal religious observances and hold a ceremony which is typically Catholic, at least "Acoma Catholic." It is the time for the annual "Feast Day of Saint Stephen." Early in the morning the statue of the "saint" is taken from the altar and brought to the plaza. There it is placed in a bower of cornstalks and aspen boughs. Officers of the pueblo stay with it throughout the day. The people dance until late afternoon when the officers return the statue to the church. At this time the bells are rung and the crowd follows the leaders into the building where the statue of Saint Stephen is placed again on the altar until the following year. The public is welcomed to Saint Stephen's feast day and the Acoma people open their homes to their friends. They serve food and give presents of loaves of bread baked in the beehive ovens. It is a time of happiness and festivity for all.

The best-known craft of Acoma is pottery, and there are several shops in the pueblo where pots may be purchased. The pottery is hard and very fine in texture. Beautiful designs, both geometric and of parrotlike birds are typical. Small double-necked, ornately decorated pots are usually found in these stores and all the merchandise can be purchased for much less money than in "outside" shops.

Works are always signed, and some of the potters have attained reputations as excellent artisans. Lucy Lewis is probably the best known Acoma potter and her work is recognized worldwide.

Tourism has become an important part of the economy at Acoma. Besides the income from ceramics, tourists add to the treasury with fees for visiting the pueblo, photographic fees, and parking fees. Local food is available and refreshments can be purchased. Fishing is open to visitors from March 15 to December 15 at Mesa Hill Lake and the San Jose River. There are some motel and other facilities at the lake, and tourists are encouraged to make use of them.

As the Acoma people gain more control of their reservation and its resources, the economic condition of the tribe will undoubtedly improve. The tribe is rapidly acquiring the art of balancing between the old and the new, of acquisition of material possessions without surrendering the ancient aesthetic values, of surviving in the modern world while maintaining their traditions and spiritualism.

## LAGUNA

Forty-two miles west of Albuquerque is the Keresan-speaking Laguna Pueblo. Located on Interstate 40 (U.S. 66), it is probably seen by more Americans than any other Indian community in the country although most do not recognize it as such. The village, founded in 1697, sits on a hill adjacent to the main east-west transportation artery and is in plain view and within photographic range.

Laguna Pueblo, New Mexico

Enchanted Mesa (Corn Mountain) — Sacred sanctuary
for the Zuni Indians — Zuni Pueblo, New Mexico

Laguna is the most recent of the pueblos now occupied in New Mexico and the people are from various tribal groups. Following the Pueblo Revolt in 1680 when the Spanish were driven out, there were many changes in population in the area. In 1692, when the Spanish reoccupied the Rio Grande territory, a number of people from various pueblos fled to Acoma and took refuge on the isolated mesa. A few went on to live with the Zuni, and in 1697 the balance, along with some dissident Acoma, moved about fourteen miles northeast and established Laguna Pueblo. Laguna apparently received a grant from the Spanish Crown for their land, but the document to substantiate such a claim cannot be found. Consequently, there have been disagreements, some vocal, some legal, and one physical battle between Acoma and Laguna over the location of the boundary separating the two reservations. It was not until 1884 that the United States established the present lines delineating the extent of the land holdings of the two pueblos.

The religious traditions at Laguna are Pueblo, but, with the people being from various segments of Pueblo society and some rituals and ceremonies having been "borrowed" from Zuni and Acoma and others, they are quite varied. Each religious or medicine society is known for some special purpose, but all groups participate in all the major ceremonies. Today, most ceremonials are seldom observed, for Laguna has become the most affluent and acculturated of all the pueblos. Interest has been expressed recently in reviving the old ceremonies, but the hierarchy is gone and most Laguna have totally adapted to the contemporary scene.

The political government of the pueblo is operated according to a modern constitution, and the paid secular leaders make all decisions affecting the reservation. Laguna operates along the same patterns as other rural New Mexico communities with little regard to traditional pueblo political tradition.

At one time, Laguna artisans produced quantities of excellent pottery, basketry, and woven merchandise. Today, perhaps because of the affluence due to the discovery of uranium deposits on Laguna land in the early 1950s, there are practically no crafts or handmade items available in the pueblo. Although a few people are engaged in agriculture, most of the economic input depends on uranium leases, wages earned in the mines, and employment in the commercial and social installations in the vicinity.

Though Laguna and other Indian communities nearby have profited monetarily from the uranium mines, they have suffered severe losses in human resources through death and deformity. Exposure to the radioactive materials without adequate protection is taking a disastrous toll. Not only is the current generation being affected by the rays from the deadly mineral but, perhaps, the heaviest burden may be in genetic damage to future generations of Indians. Many of the traditional tribal people are urging that the pursuit of material possessions be discontinued and the return be made to a spiritual way of life as the only chance for survival for the pueblo and its people.

# 9
# The Rio Grande Pueblos

Nineteen Indian pueblos in New Mexico are referred to as the Rio Grande Pueblos. As we have seen, several are not on the Rio Grande but are situated close to it or its tributaries. A few are quite a distance from the river and have never been dependent on its water. Since we have already dealt with the three westernmost of these, this chapter will focus on the remaining sixteen.

The northern pueblos are Taos, Picuris, Nambe, Pojoaque, San Juan, San Ildefonso, Santa Clara, and Tesuque. The southern pueblos are San Felipe, Cochiti, Sandia, Jemez, Zia, Santa Ana, Santo Domingo and Isleta. The pueblos of Zuni, Acoma, and Laguna also belong to the southern group. Each of these groups has councils which cooperatively operate the programs of their respective areas, and which in turn make up the membership of the All Pueblo Council which handles affairs effecting the entire nineteen communities.

The history of these pueblo people goes back perhaps 5000 years or more to the early Basketmaker culture of the Southwest.

Evolution of the cultures occurred and the Basketmaker advanced to the Anasazi and on to the Pueblo. Changes took place and new people appeared along the Rio Grande drainage basin. Some of these came from great centers of civilization such as Chaco Canyon and Mesa Verde, others came from small settlements which existed autonomously. Why they came has never been totally documented, but various elements have been theorized as the cause. The great drought of 1276–99, the erosion of arroyos which affected food production, or the entry into the Southwest of nomadic tribes from the north — any or all of these could have been involved in initiating the immigration.

By the time the first Europeans reached the region, most of the current pueblos were in their present location. There were numerous others which were depopulated and eradicated by the Spanish and other outside influences. There are some facets of life which are common to all the pueblos, such as housing style and the tradition of living in a small village situation. The nineteen pueblos share a common traditional native religion, although rituals and observances vary, and a common economy based on the same geographic region occupied by them for thousands of years. But each pueblo retains its distinctive autonomy making it an identifiable entity in its own right.

The languages vary greatly within the pueblos, and even those coming from the same linguistic stock differ in dialects spoken by related groups. These languages belong to three basic language families — Tanoan, Keresan, and Zunian. The Tanoan language is subdivided into three dialects which, although related, are quite distinct. Tiwa is spoken at the pueblos of Taos, Picuris, Sandia, and Isleta; the Tewa dialect is native to the San Juan, Santa Clara, San Ildefonso, Nambe, Tesuque, and Pojoaque pueblos; while the pueblo of Jemez is the only one to speak Towa. Keresan is the language of the Acoma, Cochiti, Laguna, San Felipe, Santa Ana, Santo Domingo, and Zia pueblos. The third language group, Zunian, is unique and not related to any other known language and is spoken only by the Zuni people.[27]

Throughout their association with the Spanish, the Mexicans, and then the Americans, the pueblo people have exhibited a friendly, nonagressive nature and, aside from the armed defense of their homes against the ruthless Spaniards and the Pueblo Revolt of 1680, have striven for peace with all men. In the two incidents mentioned, puebloans exhibited restraint even in warfare and limited their military activity to attempts to protect and preserve their traditional way of life.

This does not infer, however, that these peaceful people are not extremely resolute when important issues are faced. In the 1680 conflict, they relentlessly drove the Spanish from their lands, but did so with little retaliatory action. Their insistence in maintaining integrity has been illustrated also in nonmilitary incidents.

A number of years ago the Santo Domingo people and a Roman Catholic archbishop came to an impasse over some of the practices of the ancient pueblo religion. The rule of secrecy is inviolable and, therefore, contrary to Catholic doctrine which demands confession. The Indians politely continued to decline to confess as their people had done since the first missionary contact. This angered the clergyman and he withdrew all Christian services from the pueblo and, in effect, excommunicated the people.

Since the parts of Christianity these puebloans had accepted were very dear to them, their services continued uninterrupted. In place of ordained white priests, they were conducted by lay Indian clergy. It took several years of this passive persistence before the archbishop got the message; the Indians would not change. Eventually, white priests returned to their posts and to this day, Santo Domingo Indians do not attend confession.

Some of the pueblos have suffered severe indignities because they would not compromise their principles and because their integrity was so strong. In the 1920s, the Taos Pueblo came under strong pressure from the Bureau of Indian Affairs through tactics which were deplorable.[28] Again, the puebloans quietly but firmly stood their ground and would not be changed. The Bureau refused to allow Taos boys to attend initiation ceremonies, an extremely important facet of pueblo culture and religion. The Taos pueblo unanimously agreed that the ceremonies would continue, no matter what penalty they suffered. The entire governing body of Taos Pueblo was thrown into prison for violating the Religious Crime Code of the Bureau of Indian Affairs. But, the ceremonies were conducted!

Many other nefarious plots and schemes were perpetrated against the pueblo people in efforts to steal their land, suppress their native religious practices, and to control their lives. Nearly all of these insidious activities were violations of their civil rights and showed a blatant disregard for the Constitutional provisions and moral and legal guidelines upon which this country was founded.

And yet, the pueblo persisted and today are enjoying a spiritual uplifting and an economic resurgence which is in keeping with the "self-determination" policy articulated by the United States government and implemented by the Indian people.

Even today, though, with a degree of modernization and acculturation taking place in the pueblos, the traditional way of life is evident. Along with the roar of pick-up motors and the garish television programs, the sounds of the "Ancient Ones," the Anasazi, are still heard in the kivas and on the ceremonial dance grounds. Their voices, through the rituals and observances, still speak to the hearts of the people and direct their lives. A close observation of the pueblos will show the presence of tradition coexisting with the effects of influence from the Spanish, the Mexicans, and the Americans.

### TAOS

Perhaps none of the pueblos so graphically illustrate the cultural mix than does Taos. Located about seventy miles north of Santa Fe, Taos is three communities in one, representing the three major cultures which have so strongly affected Taos. First is the Taos Pueblo itself which is effectively separated from the other facets of the Taos community. Although the inhabitants are in nearly daily contact with their non-Indian neighbors because of economic necessity, cultural isolation of the Pueblo has been maintained. It has even been in effect with other Indians, a fact which emphasizes the degree of distance applied to non-Indians.

About three miles south of the pueblo is Taos, New Mexico, a thriving art colony since about 1898. Exploiting the unique nature of the old pueblo and the extreme traditionalism of the inhabitants, this town has become a thriving tourist attraction. Located there are museums, art galleries, shrines, ski resorts, and curio shops which capitalize on the pueblo and separate many tourists from their coin as the Indians silently and stoically observe. The same attitude is prevalent at Ranchos de Taos, located another three miles farther south. The Indians are seemingly an integral part of this bizarre commercialism during the day, but in the evening they peacefully retire to their beloved pueblo where they live totally detached from the "rat race." Their homes are as they have been for centuries – without electricity, running water, or toilet facilities, and with an aura of peace and contentment. The people exist in two worlds while living in one, and they fail to see the validity of changing their ways.

Taos has endured over 400 years of extreme pressures from outside sources, and is still experiencing the problems imposed by encroaching American tourism. The people possess a strong and resilient culture, however, and will endure.

## PICURIS

This small pueblo, although it has been in existence since the twelfth century, is one of the lesser known of all the Rio Grande Pueblos. It is small and off the well-traveled roads, and trade and ceremonial activities are shared with Taos, their nearest neighbor. At one time Picuris was the largest of the pueblos, but revolutions, a period of exile (1696–1706), and integration with other Indians has drastically reduced the size.

This decrease in population along with Americanization of children through education, has brought the Pueblo to a position not too dissimilar to that of many rural New Mexico communities. Some "Indian" activity is noted, such as pottery making and ceremonial dress, but most of the economic scene is dominated by federal projects and state assistance programs. In general, the pueblo has shifted from a spiritual to a secular orientation with elected officials. Community buildings have replaced the kiva as the focus of community activities.

In spite of this situation, recent years have brought a revival of Picuris traditional activities among the residents of the pueblo. Additions to San Lorenzo's Day, a Catholic-Indian festival, have indicated this resurgence. The Mountain Dance is now held in late September and the Water Clown Association, a kachina society, has been revived. Social dances are held occasionally, and other culturally oriented activities are beginning to appear on the social calendar.

Less than twenty-percent of the tribal income comes from wages and crafts, but Picuris is making an attempt to participate in the rapidly growing tourist industry. Perhaps as they utilize some of the natural resources of the reservation to attract visitors, the Pecuris people can assist in the development of their own economic stability and replace the federal and state "soft money," in part at least, with more appropriate income from their own efforts.

## SAN JUAN

San Juan is the largest and the northernmost of the six Tewa-speaking pueblos. It is located on the banks of the Rio Grande and Rio Chama and, although it only contains about 13,000 acres, some 6,000 of these are tillable. Thus it has the potential of a highly developed agricultural reservation. In addition, a federal law passed in 1908 guarantees the pueblo enough water to irrigate all the land they want to farm.

San Juan has the distinction of being the first capital of New Mexico, established by Don Juan de Oñate in 1598. Previously it has been visited by the Coronado expedition seeking supplies and, of course, any riches the Indians might possess. Other Spaniards came and went from San Juan until the Pueblo Revolt of 1680. Their arrogance and cruel treatment provoked hatred from the natives. The final degradation took place in 1676 when forty-seven traditional pueblo religious leaders were jailed and flogged for their practice of native religious activities. Among them was Popé, under whose leadership the Pueblo Revolt was organized and implemented four years later. This drove the Spanish out of New Mexico and it remained free for twelve years.[29]   After the reconquest, Spain maintained jurisdiction over the pueblos until 1821 when Mexico won its independence and assumed control. This caused a furor for the Mexicans revamped land tenure, and instituted many changes in the lives of the people. The final obiquitous presence, which came to San Juan because of the Mexican Cession in 1848, has been that of the United States government. The strategies of this entity, practiced very subtly and insidiously, have been oriented toward the same goal as those of the early Spanish conquistadores; subjugation of the people and exclusion of them from their own resources which could make them independent.

In recent years, San Juan has begun to expand its tourist attractions. Production of excellent pottery has been increased and San Juan pottery is now in demand. Wood carving has also become dramatically more popular with visitors and they purchase large quantities of dance figures. Basketry and embroidery are also rapidly becoming trademarks of San Juan Pueblo craftspeople.

Currently the atomic installation at Los Alamos provides a large portion of the tribal income, as does employment in other governmental programs located in the pueblos. The people of San Juan, in common with many Indians today, are attempting to find the thin balance between maintaining traditional culture while structuring an economically functional unit in today's society. They are very conservative in guarding their ancient religious practices, but quite modern in their approach to business ventures.

## SANTA CLARA

Santa Clara Pueblo is located about twenty-five miles northwest of Santa Fe, just outside the town of Española. It is the third largest of the Tewa-speaking pueblos with a residential population of about 1000. The history of Santa Clara is parallel to that of the other pueblos with the Spanish, Mexican, and American governments forcing control over the people. The changes of governments had no great effect on the pueblo until the United States began suppression of native religions in the 1850s and continued until the end of the 1920s. Christian missionaries, aided by Bureau of Indian Affairs' officials conducted a "smear campaign" to turn public opinion against the Indians by using distorted and untrue stories designed to show "obscene" and "immoral" practices in the pueblo religious ceremonies. It is an accepted fact that these people maintain high morality in their culture, but this did not stop the insidious harassment by the reformers. These righteous purveyors of lies and twisted stories took children from their homes and shipped them miles away to boarding schools to acculturate them by indoctrinating them with Christianity. By prohibiting any activity judged by them to be "un-Christian," the children were to be "brainwashed" of all Indian cultural influence.

These suppressive tactics failed, and today the Santa Clarans perform their dances and celebrate their traditional religious observances as they have for centuries. Their customs are quite like those of their neighbors, and they enjoy an independence in spiritual thought which is endemic to the pueblos.

The development of arts and crafts is one of the most vibrant facets of Santa Clara life. Potters have gained fame for their production of excellent black polished pottery. Flared rims and impressed designs are common on their products, and some of the artisans, such as Flora Naranjo, have earned national recognition. Painters, such as Pablita Velarde, have also assisted in making Santa Clara one of the great centers of Indian arts and crafts.

Much of the tribal income is derived from commercial properties near Española and from pumice deposits and timber on the reservation. Recreation has also become a money-making venture and the tribe operates facilities about eleven miles west of Española. There are eight miles of fishing along Santa Clara

Creek as well as excellent picnic and camping areas to attract tourists. Fees for the use of facilities and services add substantial income to the tribal treasury.

Santa Clara has long been gifted with aggressive and effective political leaders. These men have carefully developed tribal resources for the widest possible benefit to the membership of the tribe. They have worked diligently to introduce innovative programs which would generate revenue for the tribe and jobs for the people without being socially disruptive. It is not surprising that Santa Clara has been able to progress and yet maintain the population better than most of the other Rio Grande Pueblos. The people extract the needed and wanted items from the outside world without compromising the value system and cultural integrity which maintains them spiritually and psychologically.

## SAN ILDEFONSO

San Ildefonso Pueblo with slightly more than 28,000 acres is located about twenty miles northeast of Santa Fe on the Rio Grande. It is one of the best-known of all the pueblos because of two things — the round community kiva which has been popularized through myriad photographs, and the famous Indian artist, Maria Martinez and her exquisite black pottery.

The people of San Ildefonso trace their ancestry to an area north of Mesa Verde, and their tradition states that they founded their current pueblo around A.D. 1300. Their history during the Spanish period is much like that of their neighbors, but they were fiercely independent in their rejection of Spanish jurisdiction as well as the encroachment of the Catholic Church into their native religious beliefs. One of the pueblo's chiefs, Francisco, was a leader of the Pueblo Revolt of 1680 and the residents of San Ildefonso held out against Spain's reconquest attempts until 1694, two years longer than the other pueblos. San Ildefonso also rejected Christianity and it was not until well into the nineteenth century that the first Roman Catholic Church was successfully established.

The resolute character of the people was not restricted to outside circumstances, and the same tenacity is illustrated in affairs within the tribe. This is especially true in dealings which include moietal differences between the Summer Kiva and the Winter Kiva members. Because of this disagreement, a schism developed within the pueblo over the ownership of the square kiva and the round kiva.

This disruption was caused at least in part by the moving of the town to the north a few hundred yards, and then back south. The near extermination of the Winter moiety by an influenza epidemic had definite bearing on the "feud" by the two factions, because the Winter people for many years did not have enough members to even operate their society. The entire matter has been complicated by strict loyalty of each group to their moiety and the resolute attitudes of the Indians themselves.[30] Even today, an uneasy truce is in effect and a confrontation could break out over some minor incident.[31]

The economy of San Ildefonso Pueblo has always depended to a degree on arts and crafts. Historically, as with the other pueblos, it was an agricultural society, but that economic base ceased to exist long ago. By the mid 1970s money from the sale of pottery, and wages from enterprises such as the Los Alamos atomic project supplied nearly all the tribal income. This seems to be the pattern which the people of San Ildefonso will follow in the immediate future.

## POJOAQUE

Sixteen miles north of Santa Fe lies the smallest of the six Tewa-speaking pueblos, Pojoaque. Although quite tiny and with little attention from the outside world, the village maintains its identity and keeps close ties with the other Tewa-speaking pueblos. The people conduct no ceremonies of their own but actively participate in those of their neighbors. Cultural identity is maintained in this way rather than by any internal system. Even the government of the village is secular, the last cacique (traditional leader) having died in the late 1800s.

The village is located in a commercially attractive place and it once owned much valuable land. Even today, after losing portions of their holdings through machinations of the federal government, the tribe controls a considerable frontage on U.S. 185. This area is being developed by the pueblo council and provides not only income for the tribe but jobs for the tribal members as well.

With the history of Pojoaque being much the same as most rural communities of Indians in New Mexico, there are no great events to relate. The people suffered from the same depredations by the Spanish as their neighbors. The Mexicans followed the same treatment pattern established by their predecessors, and the Americans used their usual strategy of usurping any valuable land, and by using the biased judicial system whenever necessary to effect their ends. These pressures forced a total evacuation of the village about 1912 and it remained unoccupied until about 1934.

Antonio Jose Tapia returned to Pojoaque in the early 1930s and, with the assistance of a few other puebloans, used the same judicial system which had corrupted their land claims to restore the autonomy of the pueblo. Livestock owners and land grabbers were removed, and the Pojoaque land was established and fenced. The people were reimbursed for their losses and the village was reestablished by the Indians. This was accomplished with the help of their friend John Collier, Commissioner of Indian Affairs.

With the development of commercial resources and the business acumen exhibited by its leadership, Pojoaque is rapidly becoming a center of Pueblo industry. Lacking the traditions, native arts and crafts, and the cultural attributes of the other pueblos, the people of Pojoaque feel their pueblo can borrow or share with their Tewa relatives and thus survive with the desired values from both Anglo and Indian perspectives.

## NAMBE

Another of the Eight Northern Pueblos is Nambe, a small Tewa-speaking pueblo located about 15 miles north of Santa Fe. It contains some 20,000 acres of land, only 300 of which is suitable for cultivation, the rest consisting of grazing land and stands of noncommercial timber.

Very little of the original native culture is seen in Nambe today. Operating without a written constitution, the officials hold councils regularly and attend to the secular needs of the village. These meetings are opened in the Tewa language, but the actual business may be conducted in Tewa or English, or both, with some Spanish used when necessary. Most of the Tewa spoken is only by the older members of the tribe. Even the traditional religious ceremonies are absent and the only rituals observed are tourist-oriented; one held on July 4, and a Catholic mass with accompanying Indian dances on October 4 to honor St. Francis.

There is little in recorded history concerning Nambe Pueblo except to generalize the treatment of the people by the Spanish, Mexicans, and Americans in the same manner as other pueblos. There were no identifiable historic events unique to Nambe, and it ebbed and flowed pretty much according to the activities of its neighbors.

Very little of the economy of the village is generated from within. A few permits or fees are required at the picnic area at Nambe Falls, and small amounts are collected for drawing, painting, or photographing. Most of the monetary gain, however, is acquired by wages earned by tribal members at governmental or commercial installations in the vicinity. In most ways, Nambe is little different than many other rural communities in the area.

## TESUQUE

The southernmost of the Eight Northern Pueblos is the Tewa-speaking Tesuque Pueblo, located almost within the northern limits of the city of Santa Fe. It is one of the few Indian communities which still operates under a strict and formal religious government. The officials who are assigned to operate the secular affairs of the pueblo are chosen annually by the village holy men.

In spite of its proximity to the urban society of Santa Fe and the apparent influence by outside cultural forces, Tesuque has remained the least known and most conservative of all the Tewa villages. Fiercely nationalistic and dedicated to complete independence and freedom, it is exemplary of traditionalism. It maintains itself as a city-state surrounded by a world it accepts graciously but only as a neighbor. As John Collier so aptly described it, "Tesuque functions when need be, and through a secondary adaptation, along the narrow edge of linear Western time."[32]

In the 1920s, Mr. Collier discovered how independent and impervious to outside pressures Tesuque remained. The government and white interlopers were relieving the people of their tribal land and the Bureau of Indian Affairs was actively engaged in eradicating their religion. Tesuque's economic production had been removed and the people were subsisting on an average of just over $16 a year, including all produce grown and eaten. When outsiders attempted to assist them, they politely declined, ignoring their physical hunger and feasting resolutely on a more lasting substitute-tribalism and tranquility brought on by the true knowledge of oneself.

With minor exceptions, Tesuque is culturally like the other Tewa pueblos. The society is divided into Winter and Summer moieties which function alternately during the year. They work in maintaining the fields, harvesting, and in directing nonsecular activities of the group. The heads of the secular government are elected by the leaders of the two moieties.

Joining in the Pueblo Revolt of 1680, Tesuque men led the first attack on the Spanish and participated in the siege of Santa Fe. Fierce in the defense of their homes, the Tesuque did not suffer from Spanish military might as much as they did from Anglo diseases, which in the eighteenth century caused population losses much greater than those suffered in battle.

Economic development is negligible at Tesuque in spite of of its geographic location and abundance of uninproved land. One of the chief reasons, of course, is the ancient Tesuque desire to remain as they are. A few attempts at commercialization have been made but these have not been outstandingly successful. Today, most of the puebloans subsist on small farming operations and wages earned off the reservation. Tourism adds little and the manufacture of the once-famous Tesuque pottery is nonexistent.

## COCHITI

About 44 miles north of Albuquerque, on the west bank of the Rio Grande, is the Keresan-speaking pueblo of Cochiti. The village site has been occupied by the Cochiti people since long before the first Spaniards' contact in the sixteenth century. The history of Cochiti follows the same general pattern of other pueblos after that time, as they were exposed first to the Spanish, then to the Mexicans, and finally to the Americans. The treatment of the natives by all three powers was one of suppression, subjugation, and exploitation, as it was with all indigenous groups of people in the New World.

The religious and political structure of this pueblo is like that of many of its neighbors, so intertwined that it is nearly impossible to differentiate between them. The secular leaders are selected by a council of spiritual headmen who act as evaluators of the appointees, with power to mete out punishment for improper conduct, even to the point of executions.[33]

Cochiti, like other pueblos, has begun to capitalize on tourism as a basic part of its economy. Although the pueblo has always had an agricultural economic structure and, even though the village is not directly on the main traffic artery, many tourists visit it each summer. Famous for the making of large, two-headed ceremonial drums fashioned from cottonwood logs, the Cochiti artisans now make smaller ones strictly for sale to visitors. Pottery, which traditionally has been of fine artistic quality, now is primarily produced only to sell and has lost some of its quality. Other Cochiti ceramic work, such as figurines, has become popular in recent years, as has beadwork and moccasin making. Cochiti men have long been known for their silverwork and produce quantities of rings, bracelets, and necklaces decorated with turquoise and other stones.

Ceremonies, some traditional and some mixed with heavy Catholicism, attract many outsiders. The kiva dances are still held, but these rituals are considered sacred and are closed to the public. Others though, such as San Antonio's Day, San Juan's Day, and the annual feast and Corn Dance on July 14, draw crowds of tourists and help fill the treasury.

Thus Cochiti, too, lives on the edge of two worlds, attempting to survive economically and still hold to the traditions which maintain psychological and spiritual security for the people.

## SANTO DOMINGO

About seven miles down the Rio Grande from Cochiti is the Keresan-speaking village of Santo Domingo. This pueblo has long been prominent in affairs affecting the area, starting with the Pueblo Revolt in 1680. One of the leaders of this insurrection was Alonjo Catiti who was instrumental in coordinating the unified efforts against the Spaniards.

Santo Domingo has been quite conservative over the years, and this has undoubtedly been the reason for the retention of their traditions. Visitors are welcome and treated with respect and courtesy if they do not abuse the hospitality or break the rules of privacy. With their many contacts with the "outside world" through tourism or their own commercial endeavors, the Santo Domingo residents have had the opportunity to experience ways of life other than their own. Being very selective, they have accepted some of the items of culture from the dominant society while maintaining a strong set of basic values and cultural mores, traits which have withstood the test of time for their people.

The political organization at Santo Domingo can accurately be termed a theocracy. The cacique, or leader of the group, is not only the secular head but also is the chief medicine man and ceremonial leader of the tribe. Each year he and the lesser leaders select the tribal political officers, which assures that the traditional and conservative posture of the pueblo will not change. In this way, Santo Domingo presents a unified stand on any issue.

Catholic Church at Santo Domingo Pubelo

Santo Domingo Trading Post just outside Santo Domingo Pueblo

The resolute and unified action was illustrated vividly when in 1956 the pueblo opposed an effort to enroll their children in public schools instead of the Bureau of Indian Affairs' schools they had attended for years. The leaders of Santo Domingo and San Felipe Pueblos kept all children out of school for the entire year rather than allow the transfer. Only after negotiation of an agreement between the pueblos, the public school district, and the Bureau guaranteeing the children rights to an education equal to the best in the State of New Mexico did the pueblo, with great reluctance, permit their children to attend public school.[34]

The ceremonies and kiva rituals at Santo Domingo are extremely sacred and are not open to the public. A series of secret societies with restricted membership also exist and are highly important to life in the pueblo. They provide leadership in the active resistance to any threat to the traditional ways or any intrusion that would tend to erode the base of established values of the tribe.

Economically, Santo Domingo has been relatively prosperous. The pueblo is quite a bit larger than many neighbors and contains a good portion of productive land, much of which is irrigated. The agricultural products, both crops and livestock, established a firm economic base.

Much of the economy is based on local arts and crafts, which in itself presents a certain paradox, for these items depend on tourism and Santo Domingo diligently pursues isolation in many matters. A number of the men travel widely to barter with those interested in their exquisite pottery, jewelry, weavings, and moccasins. Roadside booths and stands also attract tourists and are the outlet for many craft items.

Santo Domingo provides proof that it is possible in this highly technical society to extract what is desired for economic survival and to combine it with Indian values and traditions for a happy, prosperous existence.

## SAN FELIPE

Bordering Santo Domingo on the south is the land of San Felipe Pueblo. The village itself is situated at the foot of Santa Ana

Mesa, stretched along the west bank of the Rio Grande. The reservation consists of nearly 49,000 acres of land, distributed on both sides of the river, on which about 1,500 Keresan-speaking Indians reside.    According to the natives, San Felipe has been in existence since the migration of the people from their place of emergence from the underground.[35]    As far as written history records, Coronado's expedition visited San Felipe in 1540 and Spanish records indicate the current village site was established about 1700.

The San Felipe people took an active part in the Pueblo Revolt of 1680, killing some Spaniards and driving others from their territory.    However, after the reconquest of New Mexico in 1692 by the Spanish, San Felipe villagers became friends of the conquerors and suffered from the attacks of other pueblos because of this.

San Felipe is one of the most conservative of all the pueblos and follows a governmental form they claim was established by the Spirit before returning to the underground.    The cacique was assigned the task of directing all spiritual and secular activities and this mandate is still in effect.    He tends to all internal affairs of the pueblo and is the center of sacred custom and tradition.    Two war captains, with the aid of eight assistants, carry out the directives of the cacique.    These captains are selected, one from each kiva moiety, to provide equal representation.    The cacique also annually selects the secular officials, a governor, his lieutenant, eight captains, and six fiscales, to deal with the outside world.    Former officials of the pueblo comprise an advisory group for the cacique and they hold extreme power with the people.    This political structure perpetuates the conservative attitude of the pueblo.

The secret societies and matrilineal clans[36] are integral parts of San Felipe culture and social structure.    The kachina organizations present dances to bring on rain, and the various ceremonials representative of pueblo religion provide an extremely strong influence at San Felipe.

As with most puebloans, the San Felipe people are traditionally farmers but, in recent years, wage work in Albuquerque has replaced agriculture as the economic base. Although a great number of jobs are temporary or seasonal, San Felipe enjoys a comparatively high employment rate. Even though the pueblo is not noted for arts and crafts, a few artisans are engaged in various forms of basket and sandal weaving, not for tourists but for internal utilitarian use. Few attempts at any salable crafts have been made and, while tourism is extremely important to th economics of some of her neighbors, San Felipe does not rely on it to contribute to the economy.

San Felipe is interested in extracting only what is absolutely necessary for survival from the outside world. The people retain their traditional approach to life whenever possible and maintain their centuries-old, traditional sociocultural attitudes which provide psychological and spiritual security for them.

### JEMEZ

Located about twenty-five miles northwest of Bernalillo, New Mexico on the Jemez River is the Towan-speaking Jemez Pueblo. The Jemez people are the only speakers of this dialect of the Tanoan language family known to exist today. Further to the north, Jemez place-names are found which follow archaeological evidence that these people migrated to their present location and that they were once quite scattered over the northern area. Jemez oral history recounts stories of peaceful invasions of nomadic people into their former homeland and of the southward migration of the pueblo people. These nomads were, undoubtedly, the Athapaskan migrants from the Northwest.

As with other pueblos and tribes in the Southwest, the first European contact came in 1540–41 with the Coronado expedition. Following this meeting, the Jemez people were exposed to the same missionizing efforts of the Catholic Church in the seventeenth and eighteenth centuries as were other native groups.

Unlike most of the pueblos in New Mexico, Jemez's history of warfare is not restricted to the Pueblo Revolt, but is a violent one of fighting not only with the Spanish, but with the neighboring pueblos of Zia and Santa Ana.

The political organization is primarily the same as it is with many of the pueblos. The cacique heads the theocratic government, and he and his advisory council direct all operations of the pueblo. The governor and his assistants are appointed to relieve the cacique from having to deal with the outside world and to allow him to expend all his energies in directing the internal affairs of the pueblo.

The social and ceremonial organization of the Jemez Pueblo is quite similar to others discussed in this chapter. The people are divided into two moieties which are in turn subdivided into specific clans. There are secret societies and kiva rituals which tend to keep the people as a close entity and, along with the governmental structure, keep them very conservative.

Wage employment provides the major income for the people of Jemez with the agricultural tradition constantly decreasing. Some cattle-raising is done and crop-farming affiliated with that agro-industry constitutes most of the agricultural endeavors aside from gardens for home use.

Tourism is not a major factor in Jemez economy although the pueblo does have limited recreational areas, primarily for fishing. Since most of the native manufactured items such as baskets and ceramics are for utilitarian use, arts and crafts have not contributed heavily to the economy. In the past and only on occasion, Jemez potters have attempted to imitate some of the other pueblo "tourist" pottery, but with little success. Quite recently another outbreak of Jemez pottery has appeared in curio shops in the West and seems to have attracted a bit more attention. These articles though, along with a small number of baskets and woven items, are about all that are produced, and the Jemez people depend on the proximity of Albuquerque to provide most of their income through salaries and hourly wages.

## ZIA

About ten miles downstream from Jemez Pueblo is the Keresan-speaking Zia Pueblo. Little interaction between the Zians and the outside world took place until after World War II. The people were expected to live in the pueblo and keep free from outside influences which would disturb the traditional life of Zia. With the unsettling effects of the war and the encroachment on their privacy by proliferating government programs in the last four decades, Zians no longer "live as an island" and their world extends far beyond the pueblo boundaries.

During the Pueblo Revolt, Zia rose up against the Spanish, but their opposition only lasted one year. Antonio de Otermin reestablished Spanish rule over the group in 1681 with little or no resistance. Throughout the remaining Spanish period, Zia only occasionally gave any indication of hostile feelings and even assisted in military action against other pueblos until about 1700.

Zia's religious structure is quite similar to that found in other conservative pueblos. It is composed of various societies which perform their rituals according to established cycles of events. They influence the lives of pueblo members and in the past participation in the ceremonials was mandatory. Today, though, the highly Catholicized Zia people appear to be controlled more by their priest than by traditional religion and many belong to no tribal religious society.

The political organization of Zia is, as one might expect, a theocracy of the same type as that of many other pueblos. The cacique is the chief official who operates as the spiritual leader and tends to the internal pueblo affairs. Secular officials are appointed by him annually to perform the mundane tasks related to pueblo relations with non-puebloans.

Historically, Zians have been farmers, cultivating floodwater gardens along the streams and washes. Since the Spanish introduced livestock in the sixteenth and seventeenth centuries, they have tended to give up crop farming and take on sheep-raising as their principal agricultural pursuit.

Zia potters are still producing outstanding pottery with slips of white and buff with a variety of unique designs in blue, red, and yellow. The ornamentation of the pottery is quite realistic and shows both animals and plants. Zia artists, while not numerous, produce excellent paintings especially in watercolor, utilizing the particular "Pueblo" style. The sale of these products to tourists and dealers does provide some income to the pueblo and to individuals. Because of the geographic location, many Zians are employed by commercial enterprises in Albuquerque, and their wages constitute the economic base for the pueblo.

## SANTA ANA

Santa Ana Pueblo is another of the five Keresan-speaking pueblos and is situated on the Jemez River eight miles northeast of its junction with the Rio Grande, about twenty-seven miles northwest of Albuquerque. The oral tradition follows the same general pattern of other pueblos with the story of the emergence and the long migration to currently occupied territory.

The ancestors of today's Santa Ana Puebloans have occupied this site since at least the late sixteenth century when Oñate recorded the Pueblo's existence. Taking part in the Pueblo Revolt, Santa Ana was the target of Spanish cruelty several times afterward. The Spanish, the Mexicans, and then the Americans treated the Santa Anans in the same exploitive fashion as they did other Indians.

Each member of Santa Ana is involved to some extent with the religious and social entities of the pueblo. Organizations of Santa Ana parallel those of most of their counterparts, and the pueblo is divided into two moieties and numerous clans. The chief official is the cacique and he has the same near-absolute power as in other pueblos. His annual appointments assure the perpetuation of the conservative attitude and of the social and spiritual structure.

Unique with the Santa Ana religious operation is that women can be included in the masked dances, and initiation into the kachina societies is voluntary. Another feature not observed in other pueblos is that dancers keep their own masks and kachina societies are associated with medicine societies rather than moieties. As with many pueblos, some of the ceremonials are a strange mixture of traditionalism and Catholicism. All rituals, whether performed in the privacy of the kivas or not, are held to be too sacred for outsiders' participation and are closed to the public.

The Santa Ana people have always been agriculturists raising corn, beans, squash, and cotton. After the Spaniards introduced livestock, they became herdsmen, mainly raising horses, cattle, and oxen. These agricultural endeavors still supply a part of their subsistence but have gradually given way to wage work as the major source of income. The people of Santa Ana are noted craftsmen and have developed a reputation for fine weaving of cotton cloth for daily use and for ceremonial purposes. Pottery making almost died out, but there has been a revival of the art and Santa Ana ceramics of high quality are once again available. The Santa Ana puebloans have also been great traders, and for untold years they have ranged over the Southwest exchanging their merchandise for that of other tribes. Very few of these home-manufactured objects are for sale to the public and do not affect the monetary income to any appreciable degree, but they do provide merchandise from the outside world through barter.

### SANDIA

In the center of the 24,034 acre Sandia Reservation, located fifteen miles north of Albuquerque, is the small Tiwa-speaking Sandia Pueblo. Archaeological evidence indicates that Sandia Pueblo has been occupied since at least A.D. 1300. There were periods of time during the Spanish rule when the pueblo was apparently abandoned, but the people always returned. Oral tradition and Spanish history disagree on where they went and how long they stayed away. Their absence was undoubtedly brought about, though, by the presence of Spaniards in the area.

Religion at Sandia seems to follow the pattern of most other pueblos, with the two moieties, clans, and kiva ceremonials. Probably the most acculturated of all the pueblos in adoption of materials such as automobiles, running water, gas and electricity, radio and television, and other "outside" items, Sandia is the most conservative concerning the private lives of the people.

Their religious activities are not open to visitors and tourists are not openly welcomed at any time. Part of this isolationist attitude is because of the proximity to the rapidly expanding city of Albuquerque and the desire of the Sandians not to acculturate. They want to accept only the facets of American culture that they need or desire. The native religion is tremendously important to the people and is their major means of retaining their identity.

The political structure at Sandia follows the theocratic system of many other pueblos with the cacique being the spiritual and political leader of the village. He selects the governing officials and appoints them for one-year terms. They control that portion of life which deals with the outside world.

Recognized as one of the most economically stable of the pueblos, Sandia has little employment on the reservation. A few people engage in farming or herding, but most are employed in the urban area. Some pottery is produced at Sandia but craft work has little effect on the overall economic system. Unemployment is quite low and very few of the residents receive any public assistance.

Cultural distinctiveness is apparent at Sandia and it is maintained by a strong emphasis on the community, religion, language, and the restrictions imposed to combat acculturation which assures a strong Indian identity. They have been able to take advantage of the things they desire from the wider world without compromising their pueblo organization, their values, or their identity.

## ISLETA

The southernmost Rio Grande Pueblo, and the only one downstream from Albuquerque, is the Tiwa-speaking Isleta Pueblo. This village has existed since about A.D. 1200 and was actively involved with the conquistadores during the early Spanish period. The conquistadores recorded much activity in Tiquex, Spanish translation of Tiwa, from south of Isleta to north of Albuquerque and estimated that there were seventy to eighty pueblos in the area.   When the Pueblo Revolt erupted in 1680, Isleta did not join the other pueblos but, rather became the gathering point for the deposed Spaniards as they prepared for the exodus to Mexico.   These refugees, through bribery, coercion, or by some other method, acquired a party of Indians to act as bearers on their trip.   The descendants of these Tiwa Indians now inhabit the Tigua Reservation at Ysleta, Texas.   This is as far as the Spaniards could go because of political unrest in Mexico City. Thus the Indians were dismissed and for some reason chose to remain rather than return to their homeland.[37]   After the reconquest by the Spaniards, the balance of the Isletans, most of whom had sought refuge with neighbors, returned to their villages where they live today.

About 1800, a group of traditional Indians from the neighboring Laguna Pueblo left their homes because of displeasure with a "progressive" faction which had gained political power through alliances with non-Indians in the village.   Wishing to retain the ancient traditions of their people, the "conservative" members accepted the offer to settle at Isleta, agreeing to live by the laws of that pueblo and that Laguna religious objects would remain in Isleta forever.   This provision was made by the Isletans to strengthen their religious societies which had been eroded over the years by outside machinations.   The Laguna Colony became an integral part of the Pueblo and although most of the people returned to Laguna after a few years, the Kachina Chief remained behind to care for the masks and other religious articles.

The social structure in Isleta follows the same general pattern as most other pueblos with two moieties, Summer and Winter, and five subdivisions called Corn groups, sometimes called clans. These societies play an important part in the lives of individual Isletans in times of crisis and in the pueblo as a whole in seasonal activities and rituals of the two moieties.[38]

The religious organization of Isleta also follows a general procedure common to most other pueblos.   Each moiety directs the ritual requirements of its particular season and is responsible for at least one major dance each year.   The Spanish padres with their strong religious pressure, did succeed in destroying a major portion of some of Isleta's religious rituals, and only remnants of the ceremonies survive. These, however, are still included in the religious celebrations by the tribe.

The economy of Isleta Pueblo is one of the most stable and affluent of all the pueblos. The tribe has recreational facilities such as fishing, camping, and picnicking, and many tourists visit the pueblo each year. Pottery is made by the Laguna Colony but it is not of the quality of that of the northern pueblos. Some jewelry is made and sold by local artisans. There are about 5000 acres of irrigated farmland and vast areas which are available for grazing. The primary souce of income to the people of Isleta, however, comes from wages earned for work in private and governmental industries on the reservation and in nearby Albuquerque. The leasing of nearly all of the reservation land for oil testing gives promise of continued prosperity for the tribe.

Although Isleta has been fragmented to a degree and has a recognized conglomerate society, it operates quite well in the "New World" while holding fast to ancient, if somewhat synthesized traditions, which have sustained them through the ages.

# 10
# Navajo

The largest Indian tribe in the United States is the Navajo, numbering some 150,000 people. They currently reside on a huge reservation in northeast Arizona, southeast Utah, and northwest New Mexico, covering about fifteen million acres, an area about as large as the state of West Virginia. The people are Athapaskan-speaking and are said to have entered the Southwest some 1000 years ago, migrating first across the Bering Strait from Siberia and slowly spreading south and east. According to this version, they left pockets of people throughout the interior of northwestern Canada and along the Pacific coast. Linguistic and archaeological evidence lends some support and credibility to the theory.

The Navajo, or Diné as they call themselves, have another version of how they happen to be in the Southwest. Their explanation is as follows:

According to Navajo belief, the first world in times immemorial was black and had four corners. Over each corner hung a cloud column — black, white, blue, and yellow.

Creatures living in this world were Mist People, without the definite form that humans now possess. First Man was formed at the northeast corner where black cloud and white cloud met. At the same time white corn was formed, perfect in shape and full of kernels. It became the first seed corn.

At the southwest corner was the blue cloud. Where it came together with the yellow cloud, First Woman was formed. With her appeared a perfect ear of yellow corn as well as white shell and turquoise.

First Man burned a crystal which was the symbol of the mind and of clear seeing. At the same time, First Woman burned her turquoise. When they saw each other's fire in the distance, each set out to find the other. When First Man asked First Woman to come live with him, she agreed.

Meanwhile, the various kinds of Beings in the First World, the Black one, began to quarrel among themselves. As a result, the entire population moved upward into the Second World, the Blue World, through an opening in the east. They took with them all of the evils that developed in the First World.

In the Second World, the Blue one, the Insect Beings, as the Black World people were called, found many other "people." Among them were a number of Blue Feathered Beings and larger insects such as locusts and crickets. There were also badgers, foxes, wolves, wildcats, and mountain lions. These larger animals were at war with each other and causing much trouble so First Man killed some of them. Then he restored them to life after the remaining animals had given him certain songs and prayers as a reward.

When the ever-present and curious Coyote saw sorrow and suffering everywhere he went, he knew the "people" wanted to leave. When First Man learned of the situation, he tried several ways to move his people up to the next world, but he was unsuccessful. Finally, he made a magic wand of jet, turquoise, abalone, and white shell. On it he carved four footprints upon which his people could stand, and he carried them up into the Third World. In this manner they left the miseries and quarreling of the Blue World.

The Third World, called Yellow, had a great stream of water, the Female River, which crossed the land from north to south while another, the Male River, crossed from east to west. In addition, there were four major mountains. The one in the east was called Dawn of White Shell Mountain; the one to the south was Turquoise Mountain; to the west was Abalone Shell Mountain; and to the north was Jet Mountain. Turquoise Boy lived in the east, while White Shell Girl lived in the west. There was no sun.

Many other types of life existed in the Yellow World too, but all the animals were pretty much the same, for they had no form.

Although life was fairly good and excellent harvests were produced, soon trouble began. One day Turquoise Boy visited First Woman and slept with her. This was the first adultery. First Man came home and found his wife with Turquoise Boy and became very angry.

First Man then called together the leaders of the animals and men, except those who had become adulterous, to discuss the problem. They decided to separate the males from the females. They built rafts and took all the men, except the guilty ones, to the other side of the river. The women laughed saying that they did not need the men, and they would be happy without them. Besides, they still had several handsome men.

For a while things were fine. However, before long the men who had been left with the women became exhausted from trying to meet the demands of so many women. The men's desires, which earlier had been so strong, disappeared quickly.

The women began to become lazy and problems appeared. Some of them attempted to cross the river to be with the men, but the current was too strong and they were swept away and drowned. Other women used strange objects to satisfy their passions and bore many monsters and giants.

Some of the men tried to satisfy their desires in odd ways, but they were struck by lightning. By this time the women, ragged and hungry, asked the men to be taken back. The men agreed, and after a cleansing and purifying ceremony, the women were permitted to live with the men again.

Before long, heavy rains began to fall and a great flood developed. When First Man learned of the flood he told the people to come to a certain mountain. Then he took earth from each of the sacred mountains and built a higher one from which the people could climb into the next world. When it turned out not to be high enough, First Man planted a cedar tree on top. The tree grew rapidly but not tall enough for the people to climb through the sky. A pine tree likewise failed, as did a male reed. However, a female reed grew up right through the sky. The people climbed up the inside of the reed and were just able to keep ahead of the rising water. Turkey was last in line and the waters' foam reached his tail. That is why turkey tail feathers are tipped with white even to this day.

The first to enter the Fourth World was Locust, and he found only water inhabited by strange monsters. At first the monsters would not let Locust and his companions enter, but after he had passed certain tests, he and the other beings were permitted to come to the new world. Once there, they persuaded the winds to blow hard and thus dry up enough water and mud to make some land.

They started a fire using four kinds of wood. Soon afterward, First Man and First Woman taught the people how to build a hogan basically of five legs. They explained that the people must always bless their hogans with white and yellow cornmeal, as well as with pollen and with white powder made from prayer sticks. The people decided that because prayers and songs always started in the east, the hogan doorway should face east. Two types of hogans were designed, male and female, each with its own rules and uses.

It was during this time that the first person died, and it was Coyote who devised the means of deciding that the dead always go to the world below.

The sacred mountains were then remade, starting with the soil brought up from the Yellow World. To the east rose Mount Blanca (White), with Dawn Boy and several others to be its guardians. To the south was Mount Taylor (Blue) with Turquoise Boy and others living there. To the west were the San Francisco peaks (Yellow) with Yellow Corn Girl and others guarding them. To the north were the La Plata Mountains (Black) with Corn Beatle Girl and others. The white mountain was fastened to the earth with a bolt of white lightning; the blue mountain was fastened with a stone knife; the yellow mountains with a sunbeam; and the chain of black mountains held fast with a rainbow.

At this time, also, the people decided to bring order to their lives by creating night and day, and including the stars, the sun, and the moon. This they did and the world now has stars, sun, and moon. It has the various seasons which, with planting and harvesting and other seasonal activities, now bring order to peoples' lives all over the world.

The people began to move around, looking for a final place to settle. In doing this they left groups at various places which later became the Paiute, the Apache, the Hopi, and other tribes of Indians. The main party finally settled in a large area bounded by the sacred mountains where they remain to this day. They are Diné, the People, the Navajo.[39]

Although this story does not agree with archaeological explanations put forth by many authors, it satisfies the Navajo and gives logical explanation for things which are unknown. It has sufficed for centuries and will continue to do so as long as there are Navajo.

The first documented reference to the Navajo is found in a Franciscan missionary report of 1626. Shortly thereafter, another churchman wrote more about them. At this time the Navajo were composed of numerous small groups rather than one large tribe and had become sedentary and were farming and herding sheep, goats, horses, and cattle. They had adopted the agricultural concept from the Pueblo Indians and received stock, by one means or another, from the Spanish. In reports covering the first part of the eighteenth century, the Navajo had become settled and their basic raiding culture had converted to agriculture.

Even though the Navajo were originally raiders, this was not an act of hostility to them and was carried out almost as a ritual. It was their way of acquiring the material articles necessary for

Navajo hogan — traditional house style still in use on the Navajo Reservation

Canyon de Chelly — site of many Anasazi ruins on the Navajo Reservation

survival. They were even considered to be on rather friendly terms with some of the victims of their raids, such as the pueblos. During the Spanish invasion and conquest, many Pueblo people took up residence with the Navajo to escape the Spanish cruelty, and after the Pueblo Revolt of 1680 when the hated Spaniards were again rampaging through the Southwest, a number of puebloans again sought refuge with these "nomadic savages." The Hopi sought them out and lived with them in Canyon de Chelly during the droughts of the eighteenth century. This integrated life-style not only allowed the pueblo Indians to teach the Navajo their arts, such as weaving and the making of painted pottery, but they also acted as intermediaries in the transmission of various European technologies acquired by the puebloans through direct contact with the Spanish.

When the Americans took over the Southwest after the Mexican War, the Navajo were busy raising livestock, farming, trading with tribes great distances away, and doing a little raiding to keep their cultural life alive. The United States promised protection against "marauding" Indians and set out on a military program to contain the Navajo. Forts were established, Indian agents were brought in, and contracts were made with local headmen. The government did not realize that there was no central Navajo government and these headmen spoke only for their tiny bands. When these agreements were broken by Navajo outside the local jurisdiction, American authorities misunderstood Navajo social structure and judged the entire tribe to be totally untrustworthy.

Colonel Kit Carson was ordered into Navajo country in June 1863 with instructions to bring the Indians under control. The land was pillaged, livestock killed, crops destroyed, and Navajo starved. Finally the tribe was subdued and about 8000 were taken on "The Long Walk" of about 300 miles across the barren New Mexico wasteland to Fort Sumner. They were confined at Bosque Redondo, far from their beloved homeland, where they lived in a flat colorless region, ate alien foods, and drank bitter water which made them ill. They were a most miserable people and constantly pleaded with their captors to be allowed to go home.

Spider Rock in Canyon de Chelly on the Navajo Reservation

In 1868, the United States signed a treaty with the Navajo Nation[40] and allowed the people to return to their own land. And land was about all they had, for everything else was gone. Buildings had been burned, flocks had been removed, and crops and orchards had been destroyed. Their social organization of small autonomous bands had been replaced by a central government, and their entire society was changed. It was necessary for them to start anew and build from nothing.

Corrupt agents, general governmental bureaucratic bungling, and conditions over which no one had control kept the Navajo from getting their reconstruction going. The most important day in Navajo recovery finally came in November, 1869 when 14,000 sheep and 1,000 goats were driven to Fort Defiance to be distributed among the tribal members. These animals were divided equally among the 9,500 Indians counted that day, and the final distribution was three sheep, or two sheep and one goat, for every two people. Knowing the importance of the animals as the base from which the Navajo must survive and build their nation, Barboncito, the great Navajo leader, admonished his people in a speech made to the entire tribe:

> Now you are beginning again.  Take care of the sheep that have been given you as you would care for your own children. Never kill them for food.  If you are hungry, go out after the wild animals and the wild plants.  Or go without food, for you have done that before.  These few sheep must grow into flocks so that we, the People, can be as we once were.[41]

Needless to say, the Navajo did not eat their sheep and in 1872, 10,000 more animals were distributed and the Navajo had their start toward survival based on herding sheep. Today, this same base, in spite of the advanced technology of the modern world and the Navajo intrusion into it, still sustains the people.

The Navajo people have a unique way of living in the modern society of today's world without actually becoming a part of it. It is rather as if they go through the physical, everyday life protected by some invisible force-shield which wards off any attempt to include them. They remain safe and secure within themselves as long as that aura is not penetrated. They truly have acquired the ability to exist in one world and live in another.

Even the hogan, the traditional Navajo house made of mud and logs, is more than just a place to eat and sleep. It is a gift of the gods and as such, occupies a place in the sacred world. The first hogans were built by the Holy People after their emergence from the underground, and were made of turquoise, white shell, jet, and abalone shell. The hogan is round and symbolic of the sun, and its door faces east to greet the rising Father Sun, one of the most revered of the Navajo deities. After a new hogan is completed, it is consecrated with a Blessing Way ritual in which the Holy People are asked to "let this place be happy."

Everything within the hogan is prescribed by legends. The south side belongs to the women and the north side to the men. The male head of the family and any guests sit on the west side facing the door. If the hogan is struck by lightning, it is bewitched and deserted. It is also abandoned if someone dies inside. The body is not taken out the doorway, but through a hole broken in the north wall. The people are very hesitant to touch a dead person and outsiders, generally non-Navajo, are recruited to remove the corpse.

Navajo family structure is matriarchal and matrilineal, which has allowed Navajo women to be favored and more "liberated" in their society than their white counterparts. The Navajo woman owns the hogan, the land, the children, her sheep, and other livestock, her weaving and anything else which is not the personal property of her spouse. He only owns what he has inherited and whatever he has purchased from his own earnings. He may obtain a divorce by simply gathering his belongings and returning to his mother. The wife may divorce him by placing his personal property outside the hogan.

In Navajo traditional religion, there is no identifiable deity who can be described as the "Supreme Being" or " Great Spirit" as with most religious organizations. There are many powerful personages: among the most important are Changing

Woman, Sun, First Man and First Woman, Hero Twins, Monster Slayer, Born of Woman, and White Shell Woman.

The Universe, as viewed by the Navajo, is an orderly system of interrelated elements containing both good and evil. This state of good and evil must be maintained in harmony, lest bad times, sickness, or some negative concept occur. The primary purpose for Navajo ceremonials, or "sings," is to keep man in harmony with the Universe. Singers, with their specialties of two or three ceremonies, conduct the rituals to compensate for some power which is attempting to destroy the harmony and cause a traumatic situation in someone's life. The singers must specialize, for the ceremonies are many and each contain myriad songs which must be sung perfectly in tone and word. It would be impossible for one singer to render very many of these without a flaw.

The apprentice singer, usually a middle-aged man, observes and eventually aids the older singer, an honor for which he pays. Finally he might be allowed to perform a rite, but this sometimes comes only after years of dedicated study. The singer must interpret things such as an involuntary shaking of his hand or visions he receives while he is in a semitrance. From these interpretations, a cure is devised which will put the patient back in harmony. The Navajo believe that a mistake by either the singer or the patient during the ceremony can result in crippling, paralysis, or loss of sight or hearing.

The creation of a sandpainting by the singer is almost always an integral part of the ceremony. This art form is used to some degree by many southwestern tribes, but none have developed it as have the Navajo. It is made on sand or earth, or sometimes on cloth or buckskin. The figures and designs are drawn by the singer or his assistant allowing colored sand, pollen, powdered roots, stone, or bark to sift out of his hand to create the picture. Because of the sacredness of the depiction, it must be completed, used, and destroyed within a twelve-hour period.

Since the sings are nearly all restricted to the family and are of a sacred nature, photographs are forbidden. Sometimes Navajo singers do make paintings for tourists, but these have reversed colors or some other flaw built into the painting to make them less than a true reproduction of the original.

This same fraudulent reproduction is also found when Navajo tell their sacred stories to outsiders. No two versions are alike, especially with the emergence story. Each storyteller will change elements, for it would be sacrilegious to tell the accurate account to one from outside Diné. This is the reason for the many variations found in print, none of which is totally correct.

It is impossible for anyone knowledgeable of the Navajo to think of their association in a social atmosphere without fry-bread and mutton stew coming to mind. These two items, along with fried potatoes and coffee, constitute the staples in the Navajo diet. The people are also fond of and consume large quantities of soda-pop. It sometimes replaces water when it is scarce or of poor quality. Navajo ranchers who have cattle sometimes have beef to eat, and many dishes liked by the people are made from offal items and portions of the animals which are abhorrent to Anglos, such as heads, feet, tails, shanks, etc. The Navajo, as have others whose survival has been precarious, have learned to utilize everything at hand.

Beginning anew in 1868, with practically nothing and on land which at best was terrible, and after Carson's ravages left the Navajo with no sustenance, they illustrated remarkable adaptability, ingenuity, and hard work. By 1893, it is estimated that eighty-five percent of the people were supporting themselves by farming and herding. Nine percent were primarily hunters and only six percent were sustained by the government. Economically, by the white man's standards, the Navajo people are still very poor, but they have retained a remarkable degree of independence over the years.

Sheep became the mainstay in Navajo economy and for years have provided the only income for many Navajo families. The Indians, however, soon learned there was more to be realized by keeping the wool and weaving it into blankets than by selling the raw wool to traders. Selling the blankets to white tourists brought much more profit as well as establishing and publicizing the Navajo women's skills as excellent weavers.

The Navajo herdsmen became so adept at raising sheep that they soon had more than the reservation land could support. It became evident to John Collier, Commissioner of Indian Affairs, that to protect the grazing lands and assure future Navajo generations the right to follow the vocation of their forefathers, it would be necessary to reduce the size of the flocks and herds. In the mid-1930s, Collier instituted the program of stock reduction and, even today, old Navajo people talk of the time the American government "stole their sheep." The concept of Collier's plan was sound, and over the years has proven to be economically viable. However, the manner in which some portions were implemented by federal bureaucrats gave the Navajo ample reason to complain. With inadequate or inappropriate explanations to the Indians, deplorable waste of edible animals, and callous disregard for the feelings of the herders, thousands of sheep and goats were slaughtered by federal agents.

Not all abuse and exploitation of the Navajo people has been perpetrated by governmental employees though. Some of the most flagrant violations of human and civil rights are by merchants and take place on the reservation or in nearby towns. An example of this situation was publicized in 1973 in a blistering 134-page report issued by the Federal Trade Commission.[42] The FTC report indicated several bright spots in that some white traders are honest merchants who deal fairly with the Indians and try to contribute to the community, but far more frequent were instances of economic, social, and personal abuse.

The trading posts, some 150 of which are scattered around the huge reservation, are in many cases the only commercial facilities available to the geographically isolated Indian. The trader has a "captive audience" and, since they have been allowed to operate with no monitoring agency for over one hundred years, honesty and fair treatment has been left up to the individual merchant.

The trading post system on the Navajo Reservation is a unique institution, and its operation has the hallmark of a nineteenth-century general store or perhaps an early twentieth-century "company" store. It offers a comprehensive line of essential food items and manufactured articles, and purchases the Navajo wool and sheep. These are quite lucrative operations, some grossing over half a million dollars annually. They enjoy an unusual monopoly, for the Navajo live in such geographic isolation that the local trading post is generally the only accessible facility where they can procure necessary items. Patronizing another post is geographically impractical, if not impossible.

One of the most frequent and onerous abusive practices used by many traders is that of "credit saturation." This means that the post operator learns the amount of the Indian's Social Security or welfare check, and when it arrives — this is easy since most of the posts also act as a post office — the Indian's account is cleared and the endless cycle of debt starts over again.[43] Frequent instances have been documented where the trader forces the Navajo to endorse the check and never loses physical control of it, presenting it face down on the counter so the recipient does not even know the amount he is signing away. Such is the degree of economic control over the Indians.

Excessive interest rates on loans, abuses by traders when Indians pawn handmade items, low wages paid to Indian employees, and personal indignities visited upon Indians by traders are other ways Indians are mistreated at many trading posts.

Since the FTC report was rendered and hearings were held to receive testimony from some of the aggrieved Navajo, the incorporation of a Navajo legal services organization, and unpopular publicity have been the factors which have prompted some small improvements. In spite of these attempts to rectify the situation, Navajo people are still exploited and still "owe their soul to the company store" as they have for generations.

Navajo are developing into a political entity which demands recognition by county, state, and federal officials. Historically, one of the factors which helped render Indians impotent in changing their circumstances was lack of political involvement in issues which affected them. When Peter MacDonald, the first college-educated Navajo chairman, was elected in 1970, he instituted a "voter education" program to get the Navajo to use the polls as a method of bringing about needed changes in their lives.

Administration Building at Navajo Community
College — Tsaile Lake, Arizona

In the 1972 election, the Navajo astounded the State of Arizona, particularly Apache County, by electing one of their people to the post of County Supervisor. Non-Indian property-owners formed a committee which contended that the elected Navajo, Tom Shirley, was ineligible to hold the position because he, being an Indian, would be exempt from paying property taxes he might impose as a supervisor since he lived on the federally owned reservation. They filed a suit in a lower court which enjoined Shirley from taking office. The Arizona Supreme Court overruled the lower court and upheld Shirley's qualifications to take office.

As a result of the Shirley ruling, the United States Justice Department filed a suit in Federal Court in Phoenix, which will require a reapportionment of supervisory districts in Apache County. This litigation is to protect the voting rights of Indians in accordance with the "one man, one vote" guidelines. Since the county has a population of approximately 26,000 Navajo and about 6,500 non-Indians, and most of the people live in the northern, or Indian portion, that sector should have greater representation. This is not the case though, for two of the three supervisors are from the southern, or white, section of Apache County. The suit, if ruled in favor of the Justice Department, would rectify this. Thus, the committee of non-Indian ranchers could have opened a pandora's box in instituting their discriminatory legal action.[44]

The huge turnout of Navajo voters at elections held in 1974, 1976, 1978, and 1980 has had its effect on southwestern politics. Political analysts agree that the Navajo vote elected Raul Castro as Governor of Arizona in 1974, and in 1980 Senator Barry Goldwater barely was reelected because he lost the Navajo vote. In 1975 Peter MacDonald stated the situation rather succinctly when he said, "The Navajos have learned one lesson well: To get what they want, they must vote together. They learned this lesson fully for the first time last fall, in the November elections, when the Navajos turned out in such large numbers that we changed the political balance in two states."

MacDonald continued, "Once we establish out political strength, we can overcome what has been the greatest insult which Anglo society has given to all our peoples. That insult has been to ignore us."[45]

Navajo are refusing to be ignored in many facets of society. MacDonald and his economic advisors created havoc with American diplomats and bureaucrats recently by conferring with Arab oil magnates. OPEC representatives were willing to pay much more for Navajo oil than the Carter administration was willing to consider. Since the Indian tribal units in the United States are sovereign nations, it is absolutely legal for the Navajo government to negotiate contracts for the sale of their oil to foreign governments. The Navajo, with vast deposits of other minerals on their land, will undoubtedly use their prerogatives for negotiating in a wider perspective when looking for buyers in the future. Other Indians who have similar resources will also be encouraged to follow the same pattern of negotiation to obtain more equitable payments for their products.

Although huge amounts of money are poured into the Navajo reservation, they are insufficient to bring about the economic security the tribe needs. The people are still poor and the reservation is mostly a vast wasteland. Navajo have survived only by their own ingenuity, adaptability, and determination. It has only been in the last decade that Navajo futures have become brighter. With the strong concept of self-determination utilized by the Nation, there seems to be a much better day dawning for Diné, the People.

# 11
# Yaqui

The Yaqui Indians are not native to the Southwest as we know it, but rather, are immigrants from Mexico. They began to settle in Arizona about the turn of the twentieth century in an attempt to escape persecution by the Mexican government.

When first contacted by the Spanish in 1533, the Yaqui were agriculturalists, farming the lands along the Yaqui River and other streams in southern Sonora. Unlike other tribes in Mexico, the Yaqui did not accept Spanish domination and, after a number of military engagements, were able to convince the Spaniards that they would not be conquered. An uneasy peace was established and both the Yaqui and the Spanish adopted a give-and-take attitude which lasted for over a century. Each utilized approaches to issues which would be acceptable to the other without compromising their entire perspectives. The Jesuit missionaries who operated religious activities at that time acted as catalysts for the two groups, and the Yaqui voluntarily accepted a diluted version of Catholicism.[46]

After the Mexican Revolution of 1821, the relationship between the Yaqui and the Mexicans slowly began to deteriorate.
The deterioration intensified in the 1870s and by 1900, the
mutual alienation was complete.  The Yaqui were viewed by
the Mexican government as inherently warlike, lawless, bar-
barically cruel, and uncivilized.  It was thought that only force
could bring about any change in their disposition.

By this time the Yaqui had developed a stereotypic concept
of Mexicans also, at least of Sonoran Mexicans.  They were
thought to be inherently warlike, fighting constantly among
themselves, as well as with the peaceful people of the region.
They were considered basically lawless in their behavior, stealing
land, and protecting their stolen areas with military force.  It
was clear to the Yaqui that the Mexicans were created angry
and aggressive people, as natural disturbers of the peace.  In
stories they tell, they claim the Mexicans are made of the
rubbish swept aside by God, and when the first Mexican came
out of the rubbish pile, he was waving his arms and talking
loudly and threatening everyone around him.  The Yaqui even
make masks worn by "evil beings" in their Easter ceremonies
to look like Mexican soldiers.

This hatred was well founded and many Yaqui migrated to
the United States to escape the Mexican soldiers and police.
Their cruelty, along with what the Yaqui considered theft by
the government of their lands, was more than many could
bear.  The major exodus of these people from Mexico, however,
did not take place until 1905–10.

The increased demand at that time for sisal, or henequen,
fiber for ropemaking and for sugar production made recruit-
ment of peon labor in Mexico an economic necessity.  New
plantations in Yucatan needed thousands of field laborers to
produce the two products.  It therefore became common
practice to round up Indians from many tribes, especially
Yaqui, to fill the quota.  They would be shipped to hot sultry
Yucatan as slaves and worked under the most oppressive conditions.  Brutal punishment, generally whipping, was used to break
the spirits of the Indians and prevent uprisings.

During the eight or ten years of slave raids, the Yaqui suffered social disruption and moral decay. Families were broken apart and children, left without parents, were adopted by Mexicans or perhaps by other Yaqui. The Yaqui homeland was nearly devoid of native people, for those who escaped deportation to the plantations in Yucatan sought refuge in Yaqui villages which had been established in Arizona near Tucson and Phoenix.

The fate of those deported is still unknown, for in the 1930s it was reported that there were no Yaqui in Yucatan despite the thousands sent there. In Oaxaca there were a few families, but nearly all were gone from that state also. Reports indicate that large numbers of these Indians died soon after their arrival, for they were unable to survive the brutal conditions of peon life with no hope for the future.

In Arizona, because they were actually not citizens, the Yaqui squatted in small groups wherever they could find work. The two most prominent villages were Pasqua Village in Tucson, and Guadalupe Community near Tempe. Old Pasqua had been engulfed by the rapidly growing city of Tucson and most of the Yaqui have moved to New Pasqua, a 202-acre tract deeded to the tribe in 1974. This new Yaqui community has nearly one hundred homes, a community center, a church and recreational facilities.

The community of Guadalupe, also threatened with the ever-expanding Phoenix and Tempe, incorporated in 1975 to preserve its autonomy by becoming an independent town. Two other Yaqui communities, Vista del Camino in Scottsdale and Barrio Libre in Tucson, are now established.

On September 18, 1978, the Yaqui Indian Tribe was granted official recognition as an Indian tribe by the United States government. This recognition is not universal among the various branches of federal government though for the Bureau of Indian Affairs still withholds services, as each governmental unit has its own criteria of eligibility for benefits. But the Yaqui land has become a reservation and many federal programs can now be utilized for the people. To date, only the Pasqua Yaqui Association in Tucson has received this status but, for a time, other Yaqui have the option of joining the association and receiving federal services.

Many Yaqui feel this new status of federal recognition and placement as a part of the bureaucracy of the United States may represent regression. They argue that it takes away the basic independence which they fled to Arizona to obtain, and they fear the effect of government machinations on their lives if they succumb to federalization.

Yaqui culture, not widely known outside the local setting, is very much alive today on both sides of the international border.[47] The people have retained many of their social and religious values and strong family ties range between the Yaqui in both countries.

Because the Jesuit missionaries worked out a compromise with the Yaqui and did not insist on complete abandonment of the native religion, Yaqui ceremonies are a synthesis of two religions. Although Catholicism is more dominant in the rituals, traditional Yaqui religious expression is quite evident in many facets of worship. Artistic abilities, mostly pure Yaqui, are manifested in the music and art objects of these ceremonies. There are gay costumes, grotesque but brightly colored masks, unique colorful headdresses, and an array of musical instruments which are traditional with the Yaqui.

Young and old alike participate in the procession of flag bearers and acolytes during the Yaqui Easter ceremony. The pageant, dating back some 360 years, celebrates the passion of Christ and symbolizes the battle between the forces of good and evil. The procession of Judas and the Fariseo also is one of the highlights of the Easter ceremony. It is an interesting blend of Catholicism and the centuries-old Yaqui native religion.

And so the Yaqui, as are other Indians in the Southwest, are in a transitional situation and faced with the centuries-old problem of survival as a people. Over countless hundreds of years, the Indians in the Southwest have developed and evolved cultures that literally grew from Mother Earth, cultures which overcame famine, adversity, and defeat; cultures which survived. This has been the story of the people who endured; who were yesterday, are today, and will be tomorrow.

# Footnotes

1. Read William E. Coffer (Koi Hosh), *Spirits of the Sacred Mountains* (New York: Van Nostrand Reinhold Co., 1978).
2. William E. Coffer (Koi Hosh), *Where Is The Eagle?* (New York: Van Nostrand Reinhold Co., 1981).
3. For more information read Walter C. Shurling, *Pleistocene Man At Calico* (Redlands, CA: San Bernardino County Museum Association, 1979).
4. John C. McGregor, *Southwestern Archaeology* (Urbana IL: University of Illinois Press, 1965), and Joe Ben Wheat *Prehistoric People of the Northern Southwest* (Grand Canyon: Grand Canyon Natural History Association, 1963).
5. Read William E. Coffer (Koi Hosh), *Phoenix: The Decline and Rebirth of the Indian People* (New York: Van Nostrand Reinhold, 1979) p. 9.
6. Father Eusebio Kino introduced new methods of agriculture to the Indians and brought a better secular life while attempting to fill their spiritual needs.
7. As noted in Chapter 1, the Hohokam began as a unique culture around 300 B.C. The excavations of Haury indicate that it took 300–400 years for that culture to begin to utilize Ventana and leave artifacts identified positively as Hohokam.

8. The author began his teaching career at Indian Oasis School on the Papago Reservation at Sells, Arizona. Much of the information related in this chapter is field research conducted during that time.

9. See the map on the following page for more details and locations of the villages.

10. This author has observed and participated in some of the local rituals and can testify as to their effectiveness. He would guarantee, if the event were performed with a properly contrite attitude on the part of the participant, that spiritual cleansing and rejuvenation would result. In fact, no matter what the attitude, physical cleansing would definitely occur.

11. Op. cit., Coffer, *Where Is The Eagle?* pp. 67–75.

12. Ibid.

13. In relating "Pima" activities in this chapter the author has no way of separating "Pima" from the conglomerate group now identified as "Pimas." References will be made according to the concepts recognized and assigned to the tribe as a whole.

14. The Mojave Tribal Council has settled on the use of the "j" in spelling their name.

15. See Chapter 3.

16. The correct terminology for the religious organization referred to as "Mormons" is "The Church of Jesus Christ of Latter-day Saints." This group had an effect on most of the western Indian tribes since their doctrine concerning Indians is unique. See *Spirits of the Sacred Mountains,* pp. 32–35.

17. This theory is postulated by the author and is constructed from archaeological evidence, tribal oral tradition, linguistic-geographic deductions, and a large portion of logical reasoning.

18. Geronimo commanded a very small group of dissident Apache whose major "crime" was the love of freedom and the refusal to be confined to the concentration camps called reservations. These attributes are called patriotic and nationalistic loyalty when perpetrated by Americans in wartime situations. When initiated by Apache or other Indians, they were termed criminal, barbaric, or renegade activities.

19. William E. Coffer, *The Indian Historian,* "Genocide of the California Indians" (San Francisco: American Indian Historical Society, 1977), p. 8.

20. This author spent many happy times at Apache Summit, relaxing in the quiet atmosphere and listening to the stories related by his friend Robert Geronimo, the son of the famous Apache leader. The world lost a great storyteller when Robert died in 1966.

21. The Indian Reorganization Act of 1934 provided for a new form of government for the American Indian tribes. It took the recognition of traditional government away and instituted a political form patterned

after that of the United States "democratic" form. Many nations of Indians rejected this change and some are still holding out. The best situation which resulted was the presence of two governing bodies, neither of which has the people's total allegiance and therefore neither is truly representative of the people governed.

22. Many publications played this up during the mid-1970s and the public was apprised of the happenings. However, as with most situations such as this, after the first wave of stories the "new" wore off and it became "old news." It will take some bizarre occurrence for the activity to again be of interest to newsmen. Meanwhile, the Indians are still faced with the frustration of being pawns for the bureaucrats and politicians while nothing is done to settle the problem.

23. *Op. cit.,* Coffer, *Spirits of the Sacred Mountains,* p. xiv.

24. For detailed versions, read *The Zunis: Self-Portrayals,* stories provided by the Zuni Tribe, translated by Alvina Quam, and published by the University of New Mexico Press in Albuquerque.

25. It is an impossible task to provide even a cursory review of each of the Zuni cults in this manuscript. Therefore, the author describes the Kachina cult only and in no way intends the reader to assume it to be a comprehensive analysis. Bibliographic references should be used to acquire more detailed information.

26. *Op. cit.,* Coffer, *Spirits of the Sacred Mountains.*

27. The Hopi, although they are considered by many to be "Pueblo," are not counted among the Rio Grande Pueblos. They speak a dialect of the Uto-Aztecan language as indicated in Chapter 7.

28. *Op. cit.,* Coffer, *Phoenix,* pp. 135–140.

29. Read Joe S. Sando, *The Pueblo Indians* (San Francisco:  The Indian Historian Press, 1976).

30. It is an accepted fact that "Indian unity" is a rather infrequent occurrence. So much energy is spent on inter- and intratribal fighting that there is usually only a small portion directed toward the common adversary.

31. For a much clearer description, read Sandra A. Edelman, "San Ildefonso Pueblo" *Handbook of North American Indians, Volume 9, Southwest* (Washington, DC:  Smithsonian Institution, 1979), pp. 308–316.

32. John Collier, *On The Gleaming Way* (Chicago:  The Swallow Press, 1949), p. 18.

33. For more detailed descriptions, refer to the bibliographical references. Some of these are written by Puebloans, who are the only ones who totally comprehend the intricacies well enough to accurately describe them.

34. William E. Coffer, *Indian Education:  A Study in Self-determination,* Doctoral Dissertation, California Western University, 1976, p. 16.

35. A great many of the Indian tribal creation stories tell of an emergence from the underground by the people. Many also tell of migrations of great distances, fraught with severe hardships, and of the eventual

location of "their place" on the earth. For sampling of these stories read, William E. Coffer, *Spirits of the Sacred Mountains* and *Where Is The Eagle?*, published by Van Nostrand Reinhold Co., in 1978 and 1981 respectively.

36. Some pueblos are composed of matrilineal structures and some patrilineal.

37. Read Coffer, op. cit. *Phoenix*, pp. 37, 192–193.

38. For more detailed accounts of the internal organizations of the Pueblo, read Florence H. Ellis "Isleta Pueblo," *Handbook of the North American Indians Volume 9* (Washington, DC: Smithsonian Institution, 1979), pp. 351-365.

39. Coffer, op. cit., *Spirits of the Sacred Mountains,* pp. 48-52.

40. Coffer, op. cit., *Phoenix,* Appendix. A complete copy of the Navajo Treaty of 1868 is provided.

41. Ruth Underhill *Here Come the Navaho* (Washington, DC: Department of Interior, Bureau of Indian Affairs, Branch of Education, 1953), p. 190.

42. Los Angeles Regional Office, Federal Trade Commission, *The Trading Post System on the Navajo Reservation,* June 3, 1973.

43. This practice, and others outlined in this section, is not restricted to the Navajo Reservation but is common to all reservations. Because of the vast size of the Navajo and the immense amount of money involved, this reservation is highlighted.

44. The case is still buried in the courts at this writing, but legal opinions indicate the Justice Department, and in turn the Navajo, are certain to be victorious.

45. Ed Meagher, *Los Angeles Times,* "Navajo Becoming A Serious Factor in Politics," July 20, 1975.

46. The Yaqui Catholicism follows a similar pattern as the Sonoran Catholicism of the Papago people. By allowing flexibility in the functioning of the Church so as not to oppose native traditional belief, the Catholic Church was able to obtain loyalty from these people that has lasted for hundreds of years.

47. Yaqui strongholds still exist in the mountains of Mexico. These fiercely independent people can, and do if the occasion demands, exert tremendous influence on the rural villages. A few years ago, friends of this author who were traveling in southern Sonora were refused service and treated rudely by merchants in a village. When they returned to the Yaqui camp where they had been guests for a number of days and reported the incident to the leader of the group, he became quite perturbed. He sent a message to the village headman that his friends would be back in his community the next day. He further stated that if they were not received with the greatest hospitality, there would be no village the following day. Needless to say, the visitors were treated royally when they descended from the mountains again.

# Bibliography

Adams, Alexander B., *Geronimo* (New York: Berkley Publishing Company, 1972).

Arnold, Elliott, *Blood Brother* (New York: Bantam Books, 1947).

——, *The Camp Grant Massacre* (New York: Simon & Schuster, 1976).

Bailey, L. R., *The Long Walk* (Los Angeles: Westernlore Press, 1964).

Baldwin, Gordon C., *Indians of The Southwest* (New York: Capricorn Books, 1973).

Baker, Betty, *Settlers and Strangers* (New York: Macmillan Publishing Company, 1977).

Crampton, C. Gregory, *The Zunis of Cibola* (Salt Lake City UT: University of Utah Press, 1977).

Collier, John, *On The Gleaming Way* (Chicago: Sage Books, 1949).

——, *Indians of the Americas* (New York: New American Library, 1947).

Coffer, William E., *Spirits of the Sacred Mountains* (New York: Van Nostrand Reinhold Company, 1979).

——, *Phoenix: The Decline and Rebirth of the Indian People* (New York: Van Nostrand Reinhold Company, 1979).

——, *Sleeping Giants* (Washington, DC: University Press of America, 1979).

——, *Where Is The Eagle?* (New York: Van Nostrand Reinhold Company, 1981).
——, "The American Indian," *American Ethnics and Minorities* (Los Alamitos, CA: Hwong Publishing Company, 1978).

Debo, Angie, *Geronimo* (Norman, OK: University of Oklahoma Press, 1976).
——, *A History of the Indians of the United States* (Norman, OK: University of Oklahoma Press, 1970).
Dutton, Bertha P., *The Pueblos* (Englewood Cliffs, NJ: Prentice-Hall, 1975).
Dozier, Edward P., *The Pueblo Indians of North America* (New York: Holt, Rinehart & Winston, 1970).
Dobyns, Henry F. and Euler, Robert C., *Wauba Yuma's People* (Prescott, AZ: Prescott College Press, 1970).
Demente, Boye, *Visitors Guide to Arizona's Indian Reservations* (Phoenix, AZ: Phoenix Books, 1976).
Dale, Edward E., *The Indians of the Southwest* (Norman, OK: University of Oklahoma Press, 1949).

Gunnerson, Dolores A., *The Jicarilla Apaches* (DeKalb, IL: Northern Illinois University Press, 1974).

Highwater, Jamake, *Fodor's Indian America* (New York: David McKay Company, 1975).
Horgan, Paul, *The Heroic Triad* (New York: World Publishing, 1971).
Hill, Myles E. and Goff, John S., *Arizona Past and Present* (Cave Creek, AZ: Black Mountain Press, 1970).

Iliff, Flora G., *People of the Blue Water* (New York: Harper & Row, 1954).

Jacka, Jerry, *Discover Arizona Indians* (Phoenix, AZ: Arizona Highways, 1979).
Jenkins, Myra E. and Schroeder, Albert H., *A Brief History of New Mexico* (Albuquerque, NM: University of New Mexico Press, 1974).

Kluckhohn, Clyde and Leighton, Dorothea, *The Navajo* (Garden City, NY: Doubleday and Company, 1962).
Klein, Barry T., *Reference Encyclopedia of the American Indian* (Rye, NY: Todd Publications, 1973).
Keleher, William A., *Turmoil In New Mexico* (Santa Fe, NM: The Rydal Press, 1952).

Luckert, Karl W., *Navajo Mountain and Rainbow Bridge Religion* (Flagstaff, AZ: Museum of Northern Arizona, 1977).

Locke, Raymond F., *The Book of the Navajo* (Los Angeles: Mankind Publishing Company, 1976).

Lange, Charles H., *Cochiti* (Carbondale, IL: Southern Illinois University Press, 1968).

Laird, Carobeth, *The Chemehuevis* (Banning, CA: The Malki Museum Press, 1976).

———, *Encounter With An Angry God* (Banning, CA: The Malki Museum Press, 1975).

Mails, Thomas E., *The People Called Apache* (Englewood Cliffs, NJ: Prentice-Hall, Inc., 1974).

Minge, Ward A., *Acoma: Pueblo in the Sky* (Albuquerque, NM: University of New Mexico Press, 1976).

McGregor, John C., *Southwestern Archeology* (Urbana, IL: University of Illinois Press, 1965).

Navajo Tribe, *Navajoland, U.S.A.* (Window Rock, AZ: The Navajo Tribe, 1968).

Ortiz, Alfonso, *Handbook of the North American Indians* (Washington, DC: Smithsonian Institution Press, 1979), Volume 9, Southwest.

Pare, Madeline F., *Arizona Pageant* (Phoenix, AZ: Arizona Historical Foundation, 1965).

Russell, Frank, *The Pima Indians* (Tucson, AZ: University of Arizona Press, 1975).

Sonnichsen, C. L., *The Mescalero Apaches* (Norman, OK: University of Oklahoma Press, 1972).

Simmons, Leo W., *Sun Chief* (New Haven, CT: Yale University Press, 1942).

Sando, Joe S., *The Pueblo Indians* (San Francisco, CA: The Indian Historian Press, 1976).

Shaw, Anna M., *Pima Indian Legends* (Tucson, AZ: University of Arizona Press, 1968).

Spicer, Edward H., *The Yaquis* (Tucson, AZ: University of Arizona Press, 1980).

———, *Cycles of Conquest* (Tucson, AZ: University of Arizona Press, 1962).

———, *A Short History of the Indians of the United States* (New York: D. Van Nostrand Company, 1969).

Savala, Refugio, *Autobiography of A Yaqui Poet* (Tucson, AZ: University of Arizona Press, 1980).

Scrivner, Fulsum C., *Mohave People* (San Antonio, TX: The Naylor Company, 1970).

Smith, Gerald A., *The Mojaves* (Redlands, CA: San Bernardino County Museum Association, 1977).

Swanton, John R., *The Indian Tribes of North America* (Washington, DC: Smithsonian Institution Press, 1974).

Terrell, John U., *Apache Chronicle* (New York: Thomas Y. Crowell Company, 1974).

——, *The Navajos* (New York: Harper & Row, 1970).

Underhill, Ruth, *Here Come the Navajo* (Washington, DC: U. S. Department of the Interior, Bureau of Indian Affairs, 1953).

——, *Singing For Power* (Berkeley, CA: University of California Press, 1968).

——, *People of the Crimson Evening* (Washington, DC: U. S. Department of the Interior, Bureau of Indian Affairs, 1953).

Waters, Frank, *Book of the Hopi* (New York: Ballantine Books, 1963).

——, *Pumpkin Seed Point* (Chicago: Swallow Press, 1969).

Weaver, Thomas, *Indians of Arizona* (Tucson, AZ: University of Arizona Press, 1974).

Zuni People, *The Zunis* (Albuquerque, NM: University of New Mexico Press, 1972).

# Index

# Index